# NEW WEIGHT WATCHERS COMPLETE FREESTYLE COOKBOOK 2020

*TOP EASY HEALTHY & DELICIOUS WW SMART POINTS RECIPES FOR A HEALTHY DIET 3 WEEKS WEIGHT LOSS PROGRAM TO LIVE HAPPIER AND FEEL BETTER*

By

DR. CHAFFLES JOHN KETO

Copyright © 2020 Dr. Chaffles John Keto. All Rights Reserved.

No part of this publication may be reproduced, distributed, or transmitted in any form or by any means, including photocopying, recording, or other electronic or mechanical methods, or by any information storage and retrieval system without the prior written permission of the publisher, except in the case of very brief quotations embodied in critical reviews and certain other noncommercial uses permitted by copyright law.

## TABLE OF CONTENTS

INTRODUCTION .................................................................... 4

Background And History ......................................................... 6

Weight Watchers Freestyle: What It Is and how it works ...... 18

Can It Help You Lose Weight? ............................................... 30

How weight loss occurs ......................................................... 33

Weight Gain: How Food Actually Puts on Pounds ................. 37

Foods to Eat ........................................................................... 48

Foods to Avoid ....................................................................... 49

Why Is Weight Watchers So Successful? ............................... 50

Weight watchers lifestyle's diet ............................................. 53

Weight Watchers Zero-Point Foods ....................................... 54

Weight watchers Shopping List .............................................. 63

3 weeks weight watchers Meal plan ....................................... 65

Pros and cons of weight watchers lifestle ............................ 186

Benefits ................................................................................. 192

Things You Might Not Know About Weight Watchers ......... 194

CONCLUSION ....................................................................... 202

# INTRODUCTION

Weight Watchers is among the most popular weight-loss programs worldwide.

Countless people have joined it intending to lose pounds.

Weight Watchers registered over 600,000 brand-new customers in 2017 alone.

Even prominent stars like Oprah Winfrey have actually discovered weight-loss success following the program.

You might be curious regarding what makes it so popular.

Weight Watchers is a diet plan program with millions of members in over 30 different nations around the world.

It was founded by Jean Nidetch, a Brooklyn homemaker, in 1963. Nidetch and a group of buddies in Queens, NY, started meeting when a week to talk about how to drop weight.

Today, Weight Watchers is an international business and the largest business weight reduction program in the United States (U.S.). Approved by lots of doctors, it is available in numerous settings, from the regional neighborhood to the work environment and online.

The program includes regular conferences, self-help type learning sessions, group assistance, and a points system. The dieter goes for a target weight or a body mass index (BMI) of between 20 and 25, thought about the perfect range.

going to let you in on a little trick. Most popular healthy diets that are promoted for weight-loss-- from Paleo to Mediterranean and vegetarian-- share numerous of the very same basic concepts.

All involve eating whole foods (as opposed to packaged and processed) and filling your plate with quality sources of protein, healthy fats, intricate carbs, and vitamin-, mineral-, and fiber-rich vegetables. (Again, we're discussing the ones that fall someplace on the healthy spectrum, not an unhealthy crash diet like, ahem, the Grapefruit Diet.).

Nevertheless, each proposes a somewhat various course that results in fulfilling those concepts.

In this column, we'll be breaking them down for you one by one, so you can find out which (if any!) is ideal for you. We'll rapidly discuss the facts and then offer quick, actionable suggestions on how to follow the diet plan as part of a Nutritious Life.

As one of the most popular diets plans plans over the last 50 years, Weight Watchers-- or as it's currently named, WW-- has actually definitely helped some people accomplish weight-loss success. On this strategy, foods are assigned various SmartPoints values, and you're given an everyday allowance of SmartPoints to eat. You'll require to track your food every day to ensure you stay within your target variety to support your weight loss goals.

Weight Watchers has progressed a lot of times considering that its inception and the existing plan does offer advantages compared to those of the past. Point worths of foods are based on more than simply calories, and the company has actually made a targeted effort to move its focus from pounds shed to total health. Nevertheless, some people may still get captured up in focusing on numbers and constraint, instead of accepting healthy behaviors.

## Background And History

Weight Watchers started in the early 1960s. Creator Jean Nidetch invited a group of buddies to her New York City house to go over the very best approaches for dropping weight. That little group meeting progressed into a core part of current and past Weight Watchers programs.

Among her early group individuals, Al Lippert encouraged Nidetch to incorporate Weight Watchers in 1963. Lippert assisted Nidetch to do so, and business expanded rapidly. They became quite rich when the business went

Company Perspectives:

Weight Watchers has constantly believed that dieting in itself is not the be-all end-all of long-term weight management. The Weight Watchers program is a way of life oriented: teaching you how to eat healthily and enjoy yourself by being more active. Group conferences play a crucial role in motivating members to keep target without having to compromise life's simple enjoyments. Staying connected ways of staying motivated.
Secret Dates:

Secret Dates:

1963:

Weight Watchers is established.

1965:

Weight Watchers food line debuts.

1978:

H.J. Heinz Company buys Weight Watchers and divides business into three divisions, consisting of Weight Watchers International.

1997:

' 1,2,3 Success' program introduced.

1999:

Heinz sells Weight Watchers International to Artal Luxembourg.

Business History

Weight Watchers International Inc. is the biggest and most effective weight loss program in the world. Weight Watchers International has captured more than 40 percent of the weight-control market; more than a million people go to the company's weight loss classes in 30 countries around the world.

The Early Years

In 1961 Jean Nidetch was an obese, 40-year-old housewife living in Queens, New York. At 214 pounds and using a size 44 dress, Nidetch was always on a diet plan but never lost any weight. Completely discouraged by dieting fads that did not help her, she participated in a diet plan workshop used by the City Board of Health in New York City. Although she lost 20 pounds following the guidance provided, she quickly discovered her motivation diminishing. Determined to remain on her diet and reduce weight, she phoned a few overweight buddies and inquired to come to her apartment or condo. When her buddies arrived, Nidetch admitted that she had an obsession with eating cookies. Her pals not just sympathized but likewise started to share their own fascinations about food. Quickly Nidetch was setting up weekly meetings for her pals in her house. The ladies shared stories about food and provided each other support. Essential, they all began to slim down.

Within a short time, Nidetch was arranging meetings for more than 40 people in her studio apartment. Not long afterward, she began to arrange support system meetings at other individuals' homes. As increasingly more people participated in the meetings, Nidetch realized that reducing weight was not simply adhering to a diet plan, however encouraging people to support each other and change their consuming routines. One couple, Felice and Al Lippert welcomed Nidetch to speak to a group of obese good friends at their home in Baldwin Harbor. After satisfying weekly for 4 months, Al lost 40 pounds and Felice lost almost 50. Al Lippert, a product manager for a women's apparel chain, began to provide Nidetch guidance on how to organize and broaden her activities, and soon a four-person collaboration was formed amongst Nidetch and her other half, Marty, and Al and Felice Lippert. In May 1963, Weight Watchers was included and opened for organisation in Queens, New York.

The company's first public conference was held in an area located over a motion picture theater. When she started to reveal indications of tiredness, Al Lippert suggested that she choose crucial individuals who had actually lost weight themselves and had strong interaction abilities to assist her in expanding the program. Nidetch's remarkable speaking abilities and Al Lippert's genius for organization assisted raise Weight Watchers to the level of an evangelical motion.

Dynamic Growth in the Middle to Late 1960s

From 1963 to 1967, Lippert organized training programs, broadened the variety of company locations throughout the United States, and implemented a franchising system. By 1968, Weight Watchers had 102 franchises in the United States, Canada, Great Britain, Israel, and Puerto Rico. It was fairly easy for an individual to get a franchise for Weight Watchers programs. Lippert sold the territory for a very little fee, then charged the franchisee a royalty rate of ten percent on the gross income. The essential requirement was that the franchisee had actually finished from the company's programs and deflected the weight that he or she had lost. The majority of the franchisees were ladies from New York City who wanted to travel to establish a Weight Watchers franchise. This group was emotionally associated with the program and had a fantastic deal of faith in its principles; as a result, their commitment to the franchise sometimes bordered on spiritual fervor.

The late and middle 1960s saw a boom for the business. In 1965 Lippert contracted various food companies in the United States to produce Weight Watchers food lines for supermarkets and grocery shops, including low-calorie frozen entrees and dry and dairy low-calorie foods. Lippert was likewise creative in other methods. He designed a billfold that held small packages of sugar substitutes, skimmed milk, and bouillon that allowed followers of the Weight Watchers program to more easily manage their diet plan when far from home. Lippert started to sell products for use in the Weight Watchers classroom, such as postal scales to weigh food; established a joint endeavor with National Lampoon to release Weight Watchers Magazine; and opened a summer season camp for children with weight issues.

One of the business's most successful concepts, developed under the direction of Felice Lippert, was the publication of a Weight Watchers cookbook. Her very first Weight Watchers cookbook catapulted to the top of the bestseller lists and sold more than 1.5 million copies. The very first day of trading saw Weight Watchers stock shoot up from an initial price of $11 to $30.

Modifications in the 1970s

In 1973 Weight Watchers held its 15th anniversary event in Madison Square Garden in New York City. The host of previous Republican and Democratic party governmental conventions, famous boxing matches, and other historical nationwide occasions, the Garden was filled to the rafters with admirers of the Weight Watchers program. It was a far cry from the tenth anniversary event held just 5 years previously, which was kept in a high school auditorium. Although celebs in presence consisted of Bob Hope and Pearl Bailey, individuals had actually truly concerned see Jean Nidetch. She spoke until 1:30 a.m., with the crowd captivated by her motivating stories.

With the company's fast development, in 1973 Nidetch decided to resign from her position as president of Weight Watchers to devote herself entirely to public relations. Weight Watchers was not only an inspiring program that assisted individuals lose weight but an extremely successful service endeavor. Lippert and his personnel focused on the best method to attract people to Weight Watchers conferences and to offer them food, cookbooks, magazines, camps, health spas, and different other weight loss products.

By the late 1970s, however, Al Lippert had actually experienced 2 heart attacks and recognized that the incredible growth of Weight Watchers was much too fast for his little management group to handle. Yearly incomes had actually grown to roughly $50 million, and it was at this point that Lippert began searching for a larger corporate partner to assist Weight Watchers to accomplish the next level of organization and success. H.J. Heinz Company approached Lippert about acquiring Foodways National, among Weight Watchers' frozen food licensees. Heinz initially sought to combine Foodways with Ore-Ida, its own frozen food and controlled-portion entree manufacturer. Heinz management, nevertheless, soon realized that it was the Weight Watchers International brand that was important, not its licensee. As a result, Heinz got Weight Watchers and Foodways National in 1978 for approximately $100 million. Lippert remained president and chairman of the board at Weight Watchers.

In between 1978 and 1981, management at Heinz assimilated Weight Watchers into its business organization. Heinz divided the company into 3 parts: Foodways National's frozen food business was subsumed under Ore-Ida; Camargo Foods, a dressings, dry snacks, and dairy producer, and a licensee of Weight Watchers that was likewise purchased by Heinz, was combined with Heinz U.S.A.; and Weight Watchers' conference service organisation stayed Weight Watchers International. Heinz's strategy was to integrate the food organisation of Weight Watchers into its own food operations while enabling the conference service organisation to continue operating individually.

Expansion and Diversification in the 1980s

Chuck Berger, the new president of Weight Watchers International, started an aggressive strategy that consisted of an innovative program for weight loss, a better conference service, and a plan to redeem the business's franchise territories. In 1983 Berger became CEO of Weight Watchers International and, along with Andrew Barrett and Dr Les Parducci, laid the structure for a brand brand-new weight reduction diet plan. Dubbed 'Quick Start,' the diet intended to quicken the rate of weight loss during the very first 2 weeks. Launched with a well-conceived media blitz, the new program assisted in doubling the company's revenues within 2 years. Barrett, as executive vice-president, improved marketing, added new food product lines and concentrated on the way of life needs of people with weight control problems. One of his most successful ideas was the 'At Work Program,' which organized meetings for professional ladies at their workplace.

In 1982 the Weight Watchers brand name food products changed from aluminum-tray to fiberboard packaging and introduced one of the world's very first lines of microwaveable frozen food meals. In 1982 Weight Watchers Magazine had a flow of roughly 700,000 readers; by 1986, circulation had increased to more than one million. Teaming up with Time-Life's books division, Weight Watchers International developed a series of highly successful physical fitness tapes for the video market and began additional tasks for books, audiotapes, and videos in the areas of workout, weight loss, and health awareness.

By 1988, each of the three different service units of Weight Watchers was taping escalating profits. When combined, sales for the Weight Watchers companies amounted to more than $1.2 billion. Even as these figures were released, however, the weight control company was changing significantly. In 1989 and 1990, many rivals like Jenny Craig, Slim-Fast, Healthy Choice, and Nutri/System began to challenge Weight Watchers for a share of the marketplace. Throughout 1990 and 1991, after nearly seven years of increasing market share, the business unexpectedly stopped growing. Sales of Weight Watchers brand food items decreased precipitously, and even the prominent support system meetings started to fall in attendance.

In 1991 Brian Ruder, a vice-president in marketing at Heinz was worked with as the president of a newly reconstituted Weight Watchers Food Company. Ruder instantly embarked on a detailed reorganization technique, implementing brand-new sales, marketing, financing, research study, and production and advancement procedures. Within 15 months of the new company's formation, Ruder had upgraded practically half of its items. New product advancement time amounted to a simple 14 weeks, below the 22-month cycle previously followed. One line of product, low-fat, low-calorie meals called 'Smart Ones,' was an instant success. Throughout the same time, Dr Les Parducci was appointed by Heinz management as the head of Weight Watchers International. Parducci revamped the business's method for conference services by streamlining the contents of programs, moving conferences to more attractive environments, presenting more fun and intriguing materials for members, and establishing an entire brand-new line of convenience food products.

Trouble in the Mid-1990s

These modifications assisted Weight Watchers to stem defections to its rivals and revive its food sale business; the entire weight loss market suffered a decline in the mid-1990s. Weight Watchers also got some unfavorable promotion in 1993, when the Federal Trade Commission filed a match against it, declaring that it had actually engaged in misleading marketing. As a result of these occasions, presence at Weight Watchers classes dropped 20 percent in 1994 alone.

To uphold this message, Weight Watchers worked out arrangements with insurance coverage business to offer superior rebates on life insurance policies to Weight Watcher members. The company likewise made a more collective effort to reach out to guys, who had actually long been neglected by the diet industry (understandably so, nevertheless, as 95 percent of consumers were female), holding male-only classes in some of its.

In an effort to simplify the company's operations further, Heinz offered Weight Watchers Magazine (whose circulation had actually dropped substantially from its mid-1980s peak of more than a million readers) to Southern Progress Corp., a subsidiary of Time Inc., in 1996. Although these changes were not able to return Weight Watchers to its former, robust development levels, they did permit the company to stay rewarding throughout the middle of the decade.

By 1997, the diet industry's fortunes were improving. The new class of diet plan drugs had not just stopped working to become the remedy for which lots of consumers had actually hoped, but were in fact linked to significant illness. In addition, customers had found that slimming down through workout or crash diet had actually proved no simpler or more successful than the formula provided by Weight Watchers and its competitors. Weight Watchers had actually altered with the times. Recognizing that consumers still wanted to have more flexibility in the food they ate, the business unveiled its '1,2,3 Success' program. This ingenious plan assigned point worths to all foods, enabling dieters to consume whatever they selected, so long as they did not exceed the prescribed number of points. The business also hired the previous Duchess of York, Sarah Ferguson, to be its representative for the project. '1,2,3 Success' proved an incredible boon to the company, driving up attendance at its classes worldwide by almost 50 percent and improving profits substantially.

Despite this revitalization, Heinz-- in the course of a sweeping corporate reorganization-- offered Weight Watchers International to the European investment company Artal Luxembourg for $735 million in July 1999. Artal was a private investment group, which had as its sole financial investment advisor The Invus Group, Ltd. of New York; in an odd sort of synergy, Artal had likewise invested heavily in Keebler cookies and Sunshine biscuits. Talking about the sale in a news release, Heinz CEO William R. Johnson remarked, 'Weight Watchers is the gold standard in the global weight control business; however its services orientation does not fit with Heinz's long-term food growth method, and this sale allows us to focus on Weight Watchers foods and our other international food businesses.' Later in the year, Weight Watchers International bought its Weight Watchers magazine company from Southern Progress Corp., and Artal stayed positive that its marketing experience could, even more, reinforce the Weight Watchers brand. As a result, Weight Watchers International seemed well positioned to enter the 21st century.

Advancement of the Diet Plan

While Weight Watchers is known for its point system today, the initial 1960s program was a fairly easy list of limited, minimal, and endless foods. The majority of the diet's concepts were those Nidetch had picked up in a program at a weight problems center at the NYC Department of Health.

The guidelines of the original program were far more stringent than the present program. If you were following Weight Watchers in the 1960s, you 'd require to ...

Eat fish at least five times per 5

Only consume eggs a couple of times a week, and only at breakfast

Consume 3-5 servings of allowed fruit every day, but avoid "prohibited fruits" (like bananas, watermelon, and cherries).

Keep some foods off-limits, like bacon, avocado, peanut butter, and yogurt.

Throughout the 1970s and 1980s, variations on this exchange style meal plan were embraced. It wasn't until 1997 that points were introduced, which has evolved sometimes considering that. Here's a list of the various incarnations of points-based programs:

1997-- 1-2-3 Success Program, the first points system which appointed worths to foods based mostly on their caloric value.

2000-- Winning Points, a more personalized points system that did not have any food exemptions and consisted of adjustments for exercise.

2004-- Turnaround Program, which offered individuals an option of either the Core Program (a non-points based plan with a list of certified vs non-compliant foods) or The Flex Plan (points prepare that enabled consuming anything as long as it was within the daily points allowance).

2008-- Momentum Plan, a crossover in between the Core and Flex strategies that were point-based but highlighted a list of filling foods.

2010-- PointsPlus Plan, an overhaul of all the previous strategies. This attempted to deal with the fact that although an apple and a handful of potato chips may have the exact same calories, they are not nutritionally equal. The new points system took into account elements like fat, protein, carbohydrates, and fiber.

2015-- SmartPoints Plan, an update to PointsPlus that also emphasized workout with FitPoints.

2017-- WW Freestyle, a plan that broadens SmartPoints zero point foods (which do not need to be tracked) to consist of things like lean proteins. This is the strategy currently utilized today.

# WEIGHT WATCHERS FREESTYLE: WHAT IT IS AND HOW IT WORKS

It's possible you've been living under a rock if you don't understand about Weight Watchers.

Since launching in the 1960s, Weight Watchers has become an extremely popular diet plan for those looking to lose weight without absolutely eliminating whole food groups. Today, over 3.4 million individuals are subscribed to the program, which has been rated the # 1 Diet for Weight Loss by U.S. News & World Report.

The basic program depends on a point counting system now called SmartPoints (and there's an app that makes it extremely easy). It provides subscribers with a point budget based on their current weight and objectives. Different foods clock in at different points based upon their dietary makeup and point counting is supplemented by IRL weigh-ins and meetings at regional centers, which use a helpful environment filled with like-minded individuals.

Just recently, the brand revealed an upgrade to the program called Weight Watchers Freestyle. This variation of the diet is designed to give subscribers much more flexibility and flexibility by using over 200 zero SmartPoint foods, together with a rollover alternative. While veggies and fruits were constantly "free foods," this brand-new list includes lots of protein-rich choices like limitless chicken, seafood, and beans.

To account for the additional calories that may build up with these endless foods, Weight Watchers has adjusted the SmartPoints spending plans appropriately; subscribers who had 30 points will now have 23, while those who had 40 will now have 31.

The rollover feature enables users to save as much as 4 leftover points daily each week for unique occasions, like a birthday event or weekend vacation.

## How It Works

From its humble starts as a weekly weight-loss group for her buddies, Weight Watchers rapidly grew into among the most in-demand diet plan plans on the planet.

Weight Watchers utilized an exchange system where foods were counted according to servings, comparable to the diabetes exchange system.

In the 90s, it introduced a points-based system that designated worths to beverages and foods based on their fiber, fat and calorie contents.

Weight Watchers has actually upgraded the points-based system several times for many years, most just recently launching the SmartPoints system in 2015.

## The SmartPoints System

SmartPoints appoints different point values to foods based on aspects such as their calorie, sugar, protein and fat contents.

When beginning the program, each dieter is given a set amount of daily points based upon individual data like their height, age, gender and weight-loss goals.

Weight Watchers dieters are not restricted to particular foods or activities. Instead, they use a point system to monitor themselves daily. This makes them responsible for their weight-loss activities every day. Members can tape-record clever points on their mobile device.

The point system helps people reduce weight over the long term.

Points depend on sugar, fat, and protein. The greater the protein material, the lower the points gained. The higher the fat and sugar material, the more points that food has, and the less you can consume.

No foods are off limitations; dieters need to remain listed below their set daily points to reach their wanted weight.

Healthier foods are lower in points than junk foods like sweet, chips and soda.

A 230-calorie glazed-yeast donut is 10 SmartPoints, while 230 calories of yogurt topped with blueberries and granola are only 2 SmartPoints.

In 2017, Weight Watchers revamped the SmartPoints program to make it more flexible and user-friendly.

The brand-new system, called WW Freestyle, is based upon the SmartPoints system but includes over 200 foods rated zero points.

According to the Weight Watchers website, WW Freestyle makes life simpler for dieters because zero-point foods do not have actually to be weighed, determined or tracked, enabling more liberty when preparing snacks and meals.

The points encourage members to alter their dietary routines, to eat more fruit, vegetable, and lean protein, and less fatty, sugary food.

Here is an example:

an egg is worth 2 points

two tablespoons of low-fat cheddar cheese are worth 1 point

sliced tomatoes, onion and fresh herbs are worth 0 points

one tablespoon of olive oil is worth 1 point

An individual who consumes a 2-egg cheese omelet fried with olive oil and sprinkled with tomato, onion and herbs uses up 4 points. If their target for the day is 30 points, they now have 26 points left.

A person will aim to attain within a particular range of points, depending upon how heavy they are and just how much weight they require to lose.

A person who weighs 150 pounds, for instance, will intend to acquire 18 to 23 points a day. Someone who weighs over 350 pounds may aim to collect in between 32 and 37 points in a day.

Members also can get "Fit points" for activities such as cleansing, strolling, or gardening.

An etool can be utilized to tape the points digitally.

Each individual has their own day-to-day, and weekly target to fulfill in their own way, but within limits agreed.

Zero-point foods include eggs, skinless chicken, fish, beans, tofu and non-fat plain yogurt, amongst lots of other high-protein, low-calorie foods.

Before the Freestyle program, only fruits and non-starchy vegetables were rated absolutely no points.

Now, foods that are higher in protein receive a lower point value, while foods that are higher in sugar and saturated fat receive higher point worths.

Weight Watchers' new Freestyle program motivates dieters to make healthier food options instead of basing choices on how numerous points they are allocated.

**Community**

Community is essential for Weight Watchers. It offers a support network for individuals who desire to reduce weight. This, they say, is important for both short-term and long-lasting success.

The assistance system offers continuous favorable reinforcement for dieters. Trying to drop weight can be demanding; however, neighborhood support can make the procedure less overwhelming.

Weight Watchers members go to regular meetings, where they find out about nutrition and exercise, as well as having their weight-loss progress monitored.

Anybody can sign up with Weight Watchers, as long as they are at least 5 pounds (lb), or 2.3 kilograms (kg), over the minimum weight for their height.

Busy individuals who can not go to meetings can sign up to the online community.

**Coaching**

Apart from group meetings, Weight Watchers offers individually training and an individualized action strategy. An individual coach can help the private make a strategy that fits their way of life and routine.

Members can communicate with their coach by phone, e-mail, or text.

HOW PERSONAL COACHING WORKS:

As I pointed out, you initially fill out an online assessment, so that you're coach can learn more about what specific needs you have, considering that we're all special people with various lifestyles and goals.

Next, you get the option to choose your own coach. I LOVED that. There are males and females, all various ages, from various parts of the country. I picked a coach who lives here in the Pacific Northwest, who is likewise a mom running a home based business. I figured she comprehends my obstacles quite well. Likewise-- don't feel any pressure. You can change your coach at any time if you do not seem like you "click.".

-- and this is another preferred part-- you get to schedule your own training call. You can see at a glance what your coaches schedule resembles, and choose the date and time that fit into your busy life. So handy for me! And if something shows up, you can reschedule as much as 24 hours ahead of time too.

That method, if anything didn't make sense, I'd be able to ask questions right away. I even downloaded the Weight Watchers app to my iPad, so that I might access it on the go. I love this function revealed in the image above-- you can browse heaps of restaurants, to assist you in making healthy options when dining out.

My coach was SO much enjoyable to chat with-- like talking to a good old friend. She was motivating and so positive! She asked to discover what my primary difficulties were. I recognized that like so numerous other mamas; I avoid breakfast a lot because I'm so hectic. I skip a lot of meals due to being incredibly hectic. As we put together an action strategy for me this week, making sure to begin my day with something healthy is number one on the list. But-- it's a lot simpler than I believed it would be! I whipped up a bunch of healthy breakfast burritos for the freezer, so I can just warm one up quickly. And I'm in LOVE with the new Farmstyle Greek Yogurt from Tillamook! It's got lots of protein, low calories, and topped with frozen strawberries and a sprinkle of granola; it's only 4 points. It's scrumptious!

A FEW OTHER THINGS ON MY ACTION PLAN:

My coach stressed that I ought to be focused on getting begun-- don't stress so much about the end objective right now. When you believe about making a ton of modifications at once, it can be frustrating.

I'll commit to not only consuming breakfast daily, however, to stop skipping mid-day meals. With all of the seriously scrumptious recipes readily available on the website, this shouldn't be too tough either. I'm going to whip up a couple of batches of healthy soups, and measure out private parts for myself for lunches. All of their recipes look really simple too-- which is good because I'm rather kitchen area challenged:-RRB-.

I will, in fact, take a seat at the table for dinner, instead of consuming at my desk. One thing I was stressed over when it came to supper was that I'd have to make separate meals for me, and for the Mister. She assisted me in figuring out a lot of ways to make it work-- there are some awesome pasta dishes on their site. I can make half of it with meat, half without, and simply have a smaller sized portion than he does. She had lots of practical ideas!

In addition to helping me figure out what my most significant obstacles are-- my coach also praised me on the things that I'm doing. Which assists me to feel more urged and determined. I consume quite healthy foods most of the time-- not much fast food, extremely little meat, lots of fruits, and I consume TONS of water.

Your coach has been in your shoes previously-- they know that weight-loss itself isn't made complex, life is. All of us know that consuming much better foods, in smaller sized part sizes, and getting more activity in our day will result in healthy weight loss. But people, and our lives, are what's complicated. Which is why personal coaching is so awesome-- you get a real individual to help you determine a plan that will truly work for YOU. I already had some "real-life" tools to assist me out-- comfy running shoes, a brand-new fitness tracker, a new lot of healthy foods in your home. And now I have access to support at any time I need it, with my own personal Weight Watchers coach! I'm feeling truly excited about this new year-- I completely think I'll have some remarkable success!

Weight Watchers Personal Coaching and the 24/7 Expert Chat performance are the two most recent offerings from a weight loss company that continues to innovate in the area of community and assistance and individual success. The structure on the age old Weight Watchers approach of assistance networks, responsibility and reflection, the brand-new Weight Watchers Personal Coaching and 24/7 chat services take these values to the next level.

In addition to their Points and Meeting program, members of Weight Watchers Personal Coaching have, for the very first time ever, access to a totally trained dedicated weight-loss coach of their choice.

Generally, Weight Watchers has actually concentrated on long term sustainable weight reduction. It's hard to preserve a healthy lifestyle, and Weight Watchers emphasises long term changes in behaviour to promote healthy eating and exercise. With the addition of Personal Coaching, Weight Watchers has created an opportunity for members to develop an individual weight reduction program that operates in the long term, complete with goals and action steps.

New Weight Watchers Personal Coaching.

The Weight Watchers Personal Coaches are all effective Weight Watchers individuals who have actually slimmed down and have actually maintained their brand-new weight.

Members of the Weight Watchers neighborhood who sign on for Personal Coaching receive;

1:1 phone consultations.

An initial questionnaire used to supply background and a focus point for your Weight Watchers Personal Coach. This is likewise a fantastic opportunity for the member to assess difficulties, support networks, chances and objectives for their weight reduction journey.

The chance to choose their own Personal Coach, resolve their questionnaire and develop a personalised action plan.

A preliminary 30 minute phone discussion with the coach of your option and 15 minutes follow up sessions.

Unrestricted access to your Coach to develop personalised objectives, commemorate your successes, discuss your difficulties and overcome new concepts.

In addition to Personal Coaches who are offered to their signed up individuals, an additional service of a basic swimming pool of fully trained Weight Watchers coaches is available through a 24 hour, 7 days a week mobile or web chat application. They can aid with inspiration, innovative ideas and returning to the program when things go wrong. They are also a fantastic resource for establishing an understanding of the essentials of the program.

For those individuals who choose to utilize the online program, rather than attend the face-to-face meetings, the online and mobile chat (available for all mobile gadgets) with Weight Watchers coaches can aid with those hard initial questions, imaginative ideas for weight reduction plateaus and inspiration to continue, when it seems like you're going it alone. The experience and training these thousands of Weight Watchers coaches have received make them an indispensable resource readily available to all individuals.

Weight Watchers Plans

OnlinePlus - Includes New On-Demand 24/7 Expert Chat - $19.95/ Month + $20 Starter Fee

Weight Watchers completely online. Includes the new 24/7 Expert Chat function. 24/7 access to a pool of coaches online or through the Weight Watchers mobile chat app. Matched to those with about 10-20 lbs to lose.

Consists of;

24/7 Expert chat 24/7 Expert Chat - Unlimited access to a general online coach 24/7 by email and phone.

Video series Video series - A 8 week video program to inspire, teach and support

Dishes and personalized meals Recipes and customized meals - Access to a database with numerous delicious recipes and points worths.

A community of support.

Seamless activity tracking - A connection to online tracking for your activity. Weight Watchers online plus links with physical fitness gadgets, and automatically computes the points values of your day-to-day activity, making it simple to keep an eye on bonus points.

Conferences + OnlinePlus - $44.95/ Month.

In person conference with coaches, the foundation to Weight Watchers success and maybe the most tested weight reduction tool in the industry.

New Weight Watchers Personal Coaching + OnlinePlus - $54.95/ Month + $20 Starter Fee.

For the first time, our members can access a dedicated Weight Watchers-certified personal coach.

**Maintenance.**

After an initial weight-loss period, members can reach their target weight. At this moment, they enter an upkeep duration. Their day-to-day allowance boosts by 6 points, but they continue to track their food consumption and activity levels.

For 6 weeks, they gradually increase their food consumption until they are neither acquiring nor losing weight.

During these 6 weeks, there are regular weigh-ins. If a member manages to remain within 2 pounds, or 0.91 kg of their target weight throughout the 6-week period, they then end up being a "Lifetime Member.".

Lifetime Members can attend any Weight Watchers conference free of charge as long as they weigh in as soon as on a monthly basis, and do not stray from their target weight by more than 2 pounds or 0.91 kg.

Lifetime members who wander from their weight target variety need to pay weekly for conferences. They can then recover their Lifetime membership by going through the procedure again.

# CAN IT HELP YOU LOSE WEIGHT?

Weight Watchers uses a science-based method to weight loss, emphasizing the significance of portion control, food choices and slow, constant weight loss.

Unlike many fad diet plans that assure unrealistic results over short durations of time, Weight Watchers explains to members that they need to anticipate to lose .5 to 2 pounds (.23 to .9 kg) each week.

The program highlights the way of life modification and counsels members on how to make better choices by utilizing the SmartPoints system, which focuses on healthy foods.

Many studies have actually shown that Weight Watchers can help with weight-loss.

In reality, Weight Watchers commits an entire page of their website to scientific research studies supporting their program.

One research study discovered that obese individuals who were told to slim down by their medical professionals lost two times as much weight on the Weight Watchers program than those who received standard weight reduction counseling from a medical care specialist.

This research study was moneyed by Weight Watchers, information collection and analysis were collaborated by an independent research study group.

A review of 39 regulated studies discovered that individuals following the Weight Watchers program lost 2.6% more weight than individuals who got other types of therapy

Another controlled research study in over 1,200 obese adults discovered that participants who followed the Weight Watchers program for one year lost substantially more weight than those who received self-help products or quick weight-loss advice.

What's more, participants following Weight Watchers for one year were more effective at preserving their weight-loss over 2 years, compared to other groups.

WW is not a trend method, however rather a slow and consistent plan. Although the WW system has progressed over the years, it has actually always been about creating a well balanced diet, eating in small amounts, and eating the foods you want. Each food has an assigned number of points, depending upon its calorie count and just how much hydrogenated fat, sugar, and protein it consists of.

" It promotes the inclusion of a wide array of foods; for that reason it supports balance-- all foods are thought about 'legal,' to prevent sensation denied," says Susan Kraus, RD, of the Hackensack University Medical Center in New Jersey.

In November 2019, WW announced the launch of a new program that includes a personal assessment to assist tailor the ideal prepare for you. Based on your consuming routines, weight reduction objectives, and workout levels, the program will match you with color: blue, green, or purple. The three strategies still follow a points system to track food consumption; however, SmartPoints are individualized to you. Here's a closer look at each plan:

The Green Plan This uses more points than the other strategies and has more than 100 ZeroPoint foods to pick from.

Heaven Plan This plan replaced the WW Freestyle program that introduced in 2017. It falls in the middle in regards to SmartPoints and offers more than 200 ZeroPoint foods.

The Purple Plan This technique restricts the number of SmartPoints but provides access to more than 300 ZeroPoint foods, including fruits, veggies, eggs, and seafood.

On any WW plan, there are no "must-eat" foods-- the participant is in the chauffeur's seat when it comes to making menu choices. Kraus includes that the mix of tracking points, making healthy food options, and increasing activity levels will help the participant slim down.

" WW is an excellent program because it focuses on portion sizes, is well balanced, and puts the duty on the participant to make the right options, which is truly where it belongs since you are accountable for your success," says Barbara Schmidt, RD, way of life expert at Norwalk Hospital and a nutritionist in private practice in New Canaan, Connecticut. "You require to be able to live and eat various foods. You can have the dessert or that bagel, just not every day."

Weight Watchers is one of the few weight-loss programs with proven arise from randomized controlled trials, which are considered the "gold requirement" of the medical research study.

Lots of studies have shown that Weight Watchers is a reliable way to drop weight and keep it off.

## How Weight Loss Occurs

First, we need to know how weight-loss happen

Weight loss occurs when you regularly take in fewer calories than you burn every day.

Conversely, weight gain takes place when you consistently consume more calories than you burn.

Any food or beverage you consume that has calories counts towards your general calorie intake.

That stated, the variety of calories you burn each day, which is called energy or calorie expense, is a bit more complex.

Calorie expenditure is made up of the following 3 significant components:

Resting metabolic rate (RMR). This is the variety of calories your body requires to preserve typical physical functions, such as breathing and pumping blood.

Thermic effect of food (TEF). This describes the calories utilized to digest, absorb, and metabolize food.

Thermic effect of activity (TEA). These are the calories you use throughout the exercise. TEA can also consist of non-exercise activity thermogenesis (NEAT), which represents the calories used for activities like yard work and fidgeting.

If the variety of calories you consume equates to the number of calories you burn, you maintain your body weight.

If you desire to reduce weight, you should create an unfavorable calorie balance by taking in fewer calories than you burn or burning more calories through increased activity.

Weight reduction happens when you consistently take in fewer calories than you burn every day.

Factors affecting weight loss

Numerous elements impact the rate at which you lose weight. A lot of them are out of your control.

Gender

Your fat-to-muscle ratio considerably affects your ability to reduce weight.

They have a 5-- 10% lower resting metabolic rate than that of guys of the exact same height due to the fact that females normally have a higher fat-to-muscle ratio than men.

This means that ladies generally burn 5-- 10% fewer calories than guys at rest. Hence, males tend to slim down quicker than women following a diet plan equivalent in calories.

An 8-week research study including over 2,000 participants on an 800-calorie diet found that guys lost 16% more weight than women.

While guys tended to lose weight quicker than ladies, the research study did not examine gender-based differences in the ability to maintain weight loss.

Age

Among the many physical modifications that accompany aging is changes in body composition-- fat mass boosts and muscle mass decreases.

This change, together with other elements like the declining calorie requirements of your major organs, contributes to a lower RMR.

Adults over 70 years old can have RMRs that are 20-- 25% lower than those of younger grownups.

This decrease in RMR can make weight-loss progressively challenging with age.

Beginning point

Your initial body weight likewise affects how quickly you can expect to lose weight.

The amount of weight you lose, especially within the very first few weeks, tends to be proportional to your body weight.

People who are heavier will lose more pounds than individuals who are lighter. However, the rate of weight reduction tends to be similar percentage sensible.

An individual weighing 300 pounds (136 kg) might lose 10 pounds (4.5 kg) after reducing their day-to-day consumption by 500 calories for 2 weeks.

Alternatively, somebody of the exact same age and gender weighing 150 pounds (68 kg), may lose just 5 pounds (2.3 kg) following the exact same technique.

Although a heavier individual may lose double the quantity of weight, a less obese person may lose an equal portion of their body weight (10/300 = 9.7% versus 5/150 = 9.7%).

Calorie deficit

You must create a negative calorie balance to slim down. The level of this calorie deficit affects how quickly you reduce weight.

For example, consuming 500 fewer calories each day for 8 weeks will likely lead to higher weight-loss than eating 200 fewer calories each day.

Nevertheless, make certain not to make your calorie deficit too big. Doing so would not just be unsustainable but also put you at risk of nutrient deficiencies. What's more, it might make you more most likely to slim down in the form of muscle mass instead of fat mass.

Sleep

Sleep tends to be an overlooked yet vital component of weight-loss.

Persistent sleep loss can substantially hinder weight reduction and the speed at which you shed pounds.

Just one night of sleep deprivation has actually been revealed to increase your desire for high-calorie, nutrient-poor foods, such as cookies, cakes, sweet beverages, and chips.

One 2-week research study with random participants on a calorie-restricted diet plan to sleep either 5.5 or 8.5 hours each night.

Those who slept 5.5 hours lost 55% less body fat and 60% more lean body mass than those who slept 8.5 hours per night.

As a result, chronic sleep deprivation is highly connected to type 2 diabetes, obesity, cardiovascular disease, and certain cancers.

Other elements

A number of other elements can affect your weight loss rate, including:

Medications. Lots of medications, such as antidepressants and other antipsychotics, can promote weight gain or prevent weight-loss.

Medical conditions. Diseases, including anxiety and hypothyroidism, a condition in which your thyroid gland produces too few metabolism-regulating hormones, can slow weight-loss and encourage weight gain.

Household history and genes. There is a reputable hereditary part associated with individuals who are obese or obese, and it may affect weight-loss.

Yo-yo dieting. This pattern of losing and restoring weight can make weight loss increasingly challenging with each attempt, due to a decline in RMR.

Age, gender, and sleep are just a few of the many factors that impact weight-loss. Others consist of some medical conditions, your genes, and making use of particular medications.

## **WEIGHT GAIN: HOW FOOD ACTUALLY PUTS ON POUNDS**

There appears to be no end to the range of diet plans for slimming down. The Mediterranean diet plan, the Atkins diet plan and the South Beach diet plan are just a few of the weight reduction techniques that have gotten popularity in the last few years.

In spite of all that variety, all diet plans come back to one core principle.

" There's no navigating it: To lose weight, you've got to eat less," stated Dr George Blackburn of Harvard Medical School in his book "Break Through Your Set Point" (HarperCollins, 2007). "All weight-loss programs limit calories one way or another."

Calories, the standard systems of energy, are at the heart of weight reduction. Weight gain occurs when you take in more than you expend, and weight loss happens when you utilize more than you take in.

Just how much weight individual gains or loses likewise has a lot to do with the individual's metabolism the process by which the body's cells convert the calories from food into energy for bodily functions such as breathing.

How your metabolism impacts your weight

The body's metabolic process is responsible for the bulk of calories an individual uses. Nevertheless, the metabolic process occurs at various rates from person to individual. It tends to slow with age, due to the wearing down of cells in the body. As metabolism slows, people who continue to consume the same number of calories will get weight since the energy is not used as quickly. As lots of people age, their quantity of physical activity likewise tends to reduce, and weight gain becomes a lot more most likely.

By dieting, individuals restrict the calories they take in and can avoid that weight gain.

Fat contains about twice as lots of calories as an equal quantity of carbs or proteins. The evidence recommends people need to think about limiting both carbohydrates and fats to lose weight.

" Forcing scientists or the public into the juror's box to choose whether fat or carbohydrate contributes more to obesity resembles debating whether twisters are even worse than hurricanes," said Kelly Brownell and Katherine Battle Horgen, of the Yale Center for Eating and Weight Disorders, in their book "Food Fight" (McGraw-Hill, 2004). "People consume too numerous calories, which is essential to the obesity issue."

Can exercise turn fat into muscle?

While calories can be kept as fat, we know that not all big individuals simply have a great deal of fat muscle mass also increases somebody's size.

And although people talk of fat "developing into" muscle, that is not actually what occurs. Fat is a method of saving additional calories within the body. The workout uses calories, so it can decrease the amount of fat in the body. But at the same time, exercise locations stress on the body's muscles. That stress can break down the muscles at the cellular level, and as nearby cells fix them, the muscle cells can end up being enlarged.

Muscle tissue is denser than fat and needs more energy to preserve. So people with more muscle mass can take in more food-- and will make use of those calories.

Of the three aspects that represent calorie usage in a private metabolic process, digestion (which is the energy utilized to break down the food we consume) and exercise we have little control over our metabolic process and our food digestion. We can control how lots of calories go into our bodies, and we can control the amount of workout we do to utilize up excess calories.

Hidden causes of weight gain

Most likely, there's something in your life that's moved simply enough to make a difference, however not so much that you'd notice, states Alexandra Sowa, MD, a weight loss professional and medical instructor of medicine at New York University School of Medicine. "I see this all the time-- you may not step on the scale for a while, and you seem like you haven't altered anything, and all of an abrupt you go to the physician's workplace and notice you've gotten 10 or 20 pounds," she says.

That does not indicate it's your destiny to go up another size every year. Here are some of the most likely reasons for unexplained weight gain, and how to stop it in its tracks.

Your insulin levels might be out of whack.

If you've been battling weight problems for a while and none of your efforts is moving the needle, make an appointment with your doc or a weight-management MD, who can assess you for insulin resistance or prediabetes. (Your medical professional can also test you for hypothyroidism, in which your thyroid gland doesn't produce enough hormonal agent, slowing down your metabolism and potentially resulting in a small but obvious weight gain.).

" Insulin is the hormone that signals the body to pull glucose out of the blood stream and shop it in the muscles, liver, and fat," discusses Tirissa Reid, MD, an endocrinologist and weight problems medicine professional at Columbia University Medical. "But when you're obese, the cells do not acknowledge the insulin too, so the pancreas has to drain increasingly more-- sometimes 2 or three times the regular quantity-- till the cells respond." (This is also typical in women who have polycystic ovary syndrome-- a condition in which the egg follicles in the ovaries bunch together to form cysts.).

These high insulin levels keep the body in storage mode and make weight loss more hard, says Dr Reid. The start of this road is insulin resistance-- when your pancreas is working overtime, however, blood sugar levels are still normal.

Here's what you do: The most effective way to reverse this trend is to consume a diet low in refined carbs and included sugars, and to become more physically active, considering that muscles react much better to insulin when they're being used, states Dr Reid.

"People hear you require 10,000 steps each day, which sounds challenging, but you can likewise use it simply to see where you're at and make achievable boosts," Dr Reid states. Dr Sowa suggests these lower-GI food swaps: riced cauliflower instead of white rice; zucchini spirals or shirataki noodles (made from plant fiber) rather of pasta; and pumpernickel or stone-ground entire wheat bread instead of white bread or bagels.

Tension and exhaustion are throwing you off.

If you're up to during the night fretting about your aging parents, your hormonal teenagers, and the general lousy state of the world, this can affect your metabolic process. "Stress and lack of sleep can cause a waterfall of hormonal modifications that change your metabolism and affect your sense of cravings and fullness," Dr Sowa discusses.

Tension pumps up the hormonal agents' ghrelin and cortisol, which increase your cravings and can make you long for carbs; at the very same time, it dials down the hormonal agent leptin, which helps you feel full. Not surprisingly, a recent Swedish study of 3,800 ladies over 20 years found that the more stressed out you are by work, the more weight you acquire. Tension also impacts your capability to get an excellent night's sleep, and we understand that lack of sleep can also throw off your metabolic process rates and appetite cues.

Here's what you do: It's easy-- just fix the world and make everybody around you kinder and saner.

Hm, possibly not. You can manage your stress by downloading a free app such as Pacifica, which can assist you in working towards personal goals such as thinking favorably and decreasing anxiety by sending you visualizations and meditations to do throughout the day. To sleep more soundly, you already understand you need to put down your phone, computer, and iPad an hour before bedtime, but brand-new research reveals that locking out all light-- consisting of that sliver of the moon through your window-- can aid with both sleep and metabolism. A study last year at Northwestern University Feinberg School of Medicine found that after subjects spent just one night of oversleeping a space with increased light, insulin levels were considerably greater than those who overslept complete darkness, potentially affecting metabolism rates. So consider investing in some good blackout drapes.

Your allergic reaction pills are to blame.

" We're not 100% sure why, however, it's thought that histamines, chemicals produced by your body immune system, have a function in appetite control," states Dr Reid. That suggests that "antihistamines may trigger you to consume more," she says. A big study from Yale University confirmed that there is a connection between regular antihistamine usage and weight problems. Dr Reid points out that some antihistamines such as Benadryl also cause drowsiness, so if you take them routinely, you may be tempted to crash on the couch rather than go for a run, triggering more weight gain.

Here's what you can do: If you suffer from seasonal allergic reactions and are continuously taking antihistamines, speak with your specialist about alternative treatments such as nasal steroid sprays, nasal antihistamines (which have less absorption into the blood stream, and for that reason less impact on appetite), leukotriene inhibitors such as Singulair, or allergy shots, suggests Jeffrey Demain, MD, founder of the Allergy Asthma & Immunology Center of Alaska. He also says that managing your environment-- using a HEPA filter, cleaning your sheets regularly in hot water, keeping family pets out of your bed room-- can assist minimize the need for allergic reaction medications. While you're at it, do a stock of any prescription medications you're taking that are understood to trigger weight gain (including certain antidepressants, beta blockers, corticosteroids, and the contraception shot) and go over with your physician if there are equally reliable alternatives that do not cause weight gain, states Dr Reid.

Your parts are probably bigger than you think.

Anybody who's ever sat in a vinyl cubicle gazing down a bowl of pasta big enough for a toddler to swim knows that part sizes in America are ginormous. Research.

from the University of Liverpool published last year found that after being served large-size meals outside the house, people tend to serve themselves larger parts in their own cooking area approximately a week later on, indicating supersizing appears to be normalized, states Lisa R. Young, PhD, author of Finally Full, Finally Slim.

Even if your home-cooked portions have crept up just 5% over the last couple of years, that can be an additional 100 calories a day, which adds up to more than 11 pounds a year, says Lawrence Cheskin, MD, chair of nutrition and food studies at George Mason University. And the main procedure of what's a "serving" isn't helping. "The FDA standards for the number of 'servings' are in a package of food are based on how much food individuals in fact eat, not how much you ought to consume," Young describes. For instance, to show the growing appetites of the American people, a serving of ice cream was increased last year from 1/2 cup to 2/3 cup. More realistic, possibly, but still more calories than numerous of us need.

Here's what to do: First, Young suggests you spend a few days getting a reality look at how much food you're in fact consuming at each meal. "When you put the cereal in the bowl in the morning, put it back into a determining cup. What you thought was 1 cup might really be 3 cups, specifically if you're using a large bowl," she states.

Rather of relying on a federal government company (or the chef at your favorite restaurant) to tell you how much to eat, discover to listen to your own body, says Young. "Serve yourself simply one modest portion on a little plate, and when you're done, wait 20 minutes," she says.

You're consuming the ideal thing but at the incorrect time.

Let's say you switched jobs just recently, and supper is now at 9 p.m. rather of 6:30. Or your new practice of Netflixing until the wee hours also includes snacking well previous midnight. Even if you're not consuming more, per se, this modification may account for the additional poundage.

There's a fragile dance in between your circadian rhythm (the method your body and brain react to the day-to-day cues of daylight and darkness) and your calorie intake that can mean that very same sandwich or bowl of fro-yo that you consume at lunch break may really cause more of a weight gain when eaten at night. A 2017 study at Brigham & Women's Hospital discovered that when university student ate food closer to their bedtime-- and for that reason closer to when the sleep-inducing hormone melatonin was released-- they had greater portions of body fat and a greater body-mass index. Since the amount of energy your body uses to digest and metabolize food drops as your inner clock informs it to get ready to snooze, the researchers theorize that this is.

Here's what to do: There are a couple of life hacks to keep the late-night snacking to a minimum. Dr Sowa recommends you commit to jotting down every bite you eat after dinner: "Whether it's on a sticky pad or on an app, monitoring what you're consuming, how much you're eating, and how you feel when you consume it will hold you liable for the calories, and it will also help you determine if you're truly hungry or just bored," she states. She likewise recommends topping off your evening meal with a brain-and-heart-healthy tablespoon of Fish Oil. "It's a healthy fat that coats your stomach and makes you feel less starving later," she states.

Your "healthy" food is loaded with calories.

You could be consuming the cleanest, most organic, dietitian-approved variety of plant-based, or fairly farmed food, but that does not imply the calories vaporize into pixie dust when they go in your mouth.

And in reality, research has actually revealed that when you're eating something healthy-- avocados, salad, yogurt, whole grains-- the part of your brain that pays attention to fullness tends to turn off. "Even when you're consuming healthy foods, you truly have to take note of your hunger and satiety signals," says Véronique Provencher, PhD, teacher of nutrition at Université Laval in Quebec City, Canada. "In numerous research studies, we have discovered that when we perceive a portion of food as healthy, it develops a bias in our own judgment, and we believe we can eat more of it, no problem. We think a salad is healthy, so we feel we can eat as much as we desire with as lots of dressings or garnishes as we desire.".

"We have actually discovered when you are working and eating on your computer system or watching TELEVISION, or on a screen, you are detached from appetite and satiety hints," says Provencher. Something else that may help, other experts state, is to end up being more mindful of part sizes and what's in your food.

Your age may be an aspect.

Each birthday you celebrate induces one indisputable change: your basal resting metabolism (the rate at which your body at rest burns the energy you take in from food) slows down. "It's not a significant drop," states Dr Cheskin. "But as you age, you're probably also getting less active and more exhausted, and your body tends to lose muscle mass, which burns calories more efficiently than fat." Even if you're consuming the precise very same amount of food as you did when you were younger, your body is merely not burning it off as successfully as it did during the magnificence days of your 20s.

Here's what to do: You can only budge your BMR a little, but there are a few things you can do to make the mathematics work in your favor. The very first is to build up your calorie-burning muscle, states physical fitness specialist Michele Olson, PhD, a professor of sports science and physical education at Huntingdon College. "Keep up cardio three times a week for 30 minutes, however, add tough weightlifting on top of that," she states.

Olson suggests these exercises can be done at home. Start with what you can do and build as much as 2 sets of 12 of each, every other day.

Chair crouches: Sit of the edge of a chair with arms crossed; stand up and relax down for one rep.

Triceps dips: Sit on the edge of a chair, supporting yourself with your arms, slide off, strolling your feet out in front of you a couple of steps; with knees bent, and body listed below the seat, bend elbows; press up till arms are direct. (Use a chair without wheels!).

Push-ups, from your knees, or complete push-ups, if you can.

Another metabolism-boosting technique: Replace a few of the carbohydrates in your diet with proteins, which take more energy to absorb, for that reason burning more calories through diet-induced thermogenesis, as well as making you feel fuller for longer. Dr Sowa suggests you consume about 100 grams of protein over the course of the day, filling your plate with lean chicken, fish, shrimp, or plant-based proteins such as garbanzo beans, tempeh, and edamame, to give your meals more metabolism value. This might just amount to a weight-loss of a few pounds a year, however, combined with workout, the cumulative effect can be significant, says Dr Sowa.

## FOODS TO EAT

Although the Weight Watchers point system highlights whole, unprocessed foods consisting of vegetables, fruits and lean proteins, no foods are off limitations.

While healthy options are motivated, members can select any foods they want, as long as they stay under their daily SmartPoints allotment.

Weight Watchers makes healthy food more appealing to members by designating zero SmartPoints to a list of over 200 healthy foods.

Foods encouraged on the Weight Watchers strategy consist of:

Lean proteins like skinless chicken, eggs, tofu, fish, shellfish and non-fat yogurt.

Non-starchy veggies like broccoli, asparagus, greens, cauliflower and peppers.

Fresh, frozen and unsweetened canned fruit.

Healthy carbs such as sweet potatoes, brown rice, oatmeal, beans and whole-grain products.

Healthy fats like avocado, olive oil and nuts.

The Weight Watchers program encourages members to make healthy options and stresses whole foods.

## FOODS TO AVOID

While the SmartPoints system permits members to pick any food they like, Weight Watchers prevents consuming junk foods.

The Weight Watchers website recommends that members "stay with foods that are greater in protein and lower in sugar and hydrogenated fat."

Weight Watchers advises members to prevent foods high in sugar and saturated fats, consisting of:

- Sugary drinks

- Potato chips

- Processed meats

- Candy.

- Cakes and cookies.

However, Weight Watchers makes it clear that no foods are off members and limits can consume their preferred snacks and desserts as long as they remain within their designated SmartPoints.

This can be challenging for dieters that struggle with self-control and needs to be thought about when deciding if Weight Watchers is a great fit for you.

Weight Watchers motivates members to limits foods high in sugar and hydrogenated fats, though no food is off limits when following the program.

# Why Is Weight Watchers So Successful?

While there are other industrial diet plan plans that use flexibility, a range of food options, way of life changes, accountability, and long-term maintenance, Weight Watchers is one of the few to use all of them. Here's a breakdown of each part:

1. Flexibility

With the freedom to choose foods within an everyday SmartPoints goal, you can quickly modify your strategy to fit practically any age, diet, or need limitation. The capability to calculate SmartPoints using nutrition info makes it simple to include new items and dining establishment foods.

Furthermore, designating foods with point worths-- rather of calorie counts of nutrient grams-- helps keep the satisfaction of eating. Despite the fact that we're still talking numbers, SmartPoints are an abstract procedure that appears to be harder to get hung up over psychologically.

2. No Food Is Off-Limits

In previous diet evaluations I've written, namely Whole30, Keto, and carb-cycling, I've included an area about which foods are "enabled" and which to "avoid." While I comprehend the appeal of more restrictive, defined plans to customers, it goes versus the concept that any whole food can fit into a healthy diet plan. On the other hand, without a minimum of some specifications, having the ability to eat any type of food feels like practically too much flexibility.

Weight Watchers strikes the perfect balance as one of the only commercial diets to include all entire foods and food groups while developing the structure for responsibility and flexibility. This system not only makes the plan feel doable in the long-term, however it likewise avoids you from feeling guilty if you eat a slice of birthday cake every once in a while.

## 3. Focus on Lifestyle Choices

Weight and food are crucial to Weight Watchers; however, they are not the sole focus. Whether it's taking an exercise or strolling class, activity is urged and tracked through the Weight Watchers app. You can also sync the app with several popular brand names of activity screens and apps.

Furthermore, a former program called "Beyond the Scale" taught members how to have a healthier relationship with the number on the scale. By focusing on the bigger image-- adopting healthy, long-term habits and making small behavior changes to get there-- the program communicated how one's weight isn't constantly the only sign of progress.

## 4. Responsibility and Maintenance

Weekly Weight Watchers meetings and weigh-ins can help you remain on track with a weight loss objective, but the company has also recognized that this format isn't for everybody. An online version of Weight Watchers, as well as virtual one-to-one training, helps members access the very same resources from anywhere. All members, despite their plan, receive access to the Weight Watchers site, the app for activity tracking, and a big online community unique to the website and likewise on WW social media channels.

WW provides several incentives to assist you to keep the pounds off for good as soon as you reach your goal weight. In addition to offering a maintenance variation of the program, you'll likewise have the opportunity for a lifetime membership with totally free access to online tools and resources-- but only if you can keep your goal weight for a time period.

## WEIGHT WATCHERS LIFESTYLE'S DIET

Weight Watchers is a great program for anyone wanting to drop weight. The SmartPoints system makes it much easier than ever to track your food intake. You don't even need to count calories or macronutrients! There have actually been a few modifications with the Freestyle program; however, don't worry. While some point values may have altered, none of those foods has actually increased in points. In fact, a lot of your favorite foods have actually been minimized to zero points. There are over 200 zero-point foods on the list today.

Weight Watchers is an efficient and tested program for those who desire to lose weight. Dieters love the range; however, at the beginning of their weight loss journey, the quantity of food and meal choices is daunting!

One way to feel excellent about your program and narrow down your choices is to utilize a pre-arranged menu plan. Weight Watchers menus can be divided up by days and meals, and following a set strategy for a week or a month can make your life much easier. A "map" of Weight Watchers foods can be a huge aid, particularly for brand-new dieters.

# WEIGHT WATCHERS ZERO-POINT FOODS

We like the Weight Watchers points system. It not only makes it fast and simple to count calories to drop weight, but it also teaches you nutrition in the process. Something that's high in points is most likely less healthy than something that contains zero-points. I know people who used Weight Watchers to lose weight years ago, and they've effectively kept it off because of the points system! They inform me it's particularly crucial to memorize the Weight Watchers zero-point foods because these foods are "complimentary!".

The Weight Watchers program indicate foods to steer you to much healthier options. The points are assigned based on nutritional worths. "scrap food" that are filled with sugars and saturated fats aren't limited to the diet plan; however, they do have a high point worth. More healthy foods with beneficial fats and high protein contents have lower points values. You are enabled to consume a certain variety of points every day, so the choice depends on you-- feel full by consuming lots of low point foods, or satisfy your craving for sweets and consume something with great deals of points.

Under the new Freestyle program, an entire lot of Weight Watchers zero-point foods have actually been released. You can also consume nonfat yogurt without stacking up the points and lots of vegetables-- like black beans and lentils-- because these categories are all included in the Weight Watchers zero-point foods list.

As a result, these Weight Watchers zero-point foods make it much easier to produce low-point meals. You can eat numerous of them on their own as a snack or a breakfast, or you can use the supplied recipes for low-point breakfasts, lunches, or dinners.

1. Apples.

You can purchase a bag of apples and nosh on one for zero points, 2. Apricots.

This summer season fruit is among the tastiest Weight Watchers zero-point foods since it's delicious and so sweet.

3. Artichokes.

This vegetable is chock-full of nutrients, and it's also tasty.

4. Arugula.

Arugula is a spicy green that takes meals to the next level because it's easy to use and low-cost, too.

5. Asparagus.

Paleo lovers will enjoy this scrumptious Grilled Pork Chops with Asparagus and Pesto recipe due to the fact that its satisfyingly guilt-free, and it's delicious, too.

6. Banana.

A banana alone is splendidly healthy, and it's likewise a filling snack. If you have a lot of and are afraid, they'll go bad.

7. Beets.

Roast some beets for a sweet treat, and it most likely makes a fantastic side dish, too.

8. Blueberries.

A handful of blueberries may simply be sufficient to keep you away from those workplace cookies because they're fantastic at pleasing a sweet-tooth.

9. Broccoli.

This cruciferous vegetable is abundant in taste, and it's easy to eat due to the fact that it's so tasty. As a result, it's the perfect zero-point food.

10. Brussels sprouts.

A bowl of roasted Brussels sprouts alone can produce one satisfying meal due to the fact that of their taste.

11. Carrots.

Carrots on their own are a scrumptious raw Weight Watchers zero-point foods; however, they're likewise tasty when they're roasted. Need a little extra? Try these Orange Glazed Roasted Carrots.

12. Cauliflower.

This versatile veggie can take the location of rice; however, it can also be utilized instead of potatoes, meat, and more.

13. Chicken Breast.

Chicken breast is an extremely flexible protein, and it's also quite affordable. Make a huge batch, like this Slow Cooker 3-Ingredient Glazed BBQ Chicken Breasts, and use in sandwiches, salads, and more throughout the week.

14. Corn.

Kick your corn on the cob up a notch the easy way, due to the fact that this Instant Pot Corn on the Cob with Chipotle Sauce dish is so basic.

15. Cranberries.

Due to the fact that they're like nature's sweet, cranberries are tasty on their own. In addition, they're also delicious when integrated into a salad.

16. Cucumber.

Since they're filled with water and use a satisfying crunch, cucumbers are ideal for salads. Given that they're a light choice.

17. Edamame.

Sprinkle edamame with salt, and you'll also have yourself a perfectly healthy and satisfying snack.

18. Eggs.

Yes, even with the yolk, eggs are no points! Rather than preventing eggs, take your egg game to the next level by discovering some brand-new tricks and discovering How to Make Perfect Poached Eggs.

19. Eggplant.

Eggplant is one delicious food due to the fact that it's meaty in texture, rich in taste, and oh so healthy.

20. Endive.

Two absolutely no points foods come together in this Ahi Poke with Endive dish. As an outcome, you have a delicious meal that you can feel excellent about consuming.

21. Fennel.

This is a special addition to your Weight Watchers zero-point foods list. Discover fennel for the very first time in this Fennel Gratin.

22. Figs.

Figs are a sweet treat on their own, and they're likewise unbelievable when grilled.

23. Cod.

Of all, cod is a light fish that's low in calories, but it does not lack in taste, either. As much as other types of fish, you'll love the healthy taste!

24. Halibut.

Abundant halibut is a terrific method to get your protein, and it's likewise scrumptious when included with tasty veggies.

25. Salmon.

Due to the fact that it's flaky and company, tasty salmon is one mouth watering fish.

26. Tuna.

Keep your finger foods on the light side and likewise, incorporate two no points foods in this Tuna Cucumber Sandwiches recipe. They're simple and small, but most of all, delicious!

27. Garlic.

The odor of roasting garlic makes the home feel like a professional chef is developing culinary magic due to the fact that it's so mouthwatering and scrumptious.

28. Grapefruit.

This powerful and sweet fruit is fantastic by itself as a breakfast meal; however, it's also versatile, too.

29. Grapes.

They're not just crunchy, sweet, and fresh, but grapes are likewise great for you.

30. Kale.

Given that this superfood is incredibly helpful for you, you need to make it all the time! It's also scrumptious, specifically when made into a salad.

31. Lemon.

This vibrant addition to Weight Watchers zero-point foods is so versatile. Squeeze it on your salad, salmon, or in your glass of water.

32. Lentils.

Wish to keep things meat complimentary?

33. Mushrooms.

Meaty in texture, juicy in taste, and extremely tasty, mushrooms make for an excellent addition to numerous meals; however, they're likewise so terrific on their own.

34. Onions.

Required a basic, but raised, recipe making use of onions?

35. Oranges.

This juicy fruit has a lot of incredible health benefits. Considering that they're simple to find and eat, you ought to make this a primary treat!

36. Pears.

Have you ever believed of slow cooking your pears? Considering that they prepare low and slow, they become so sweet!

37. Chickpeas.

Whip up a healthy hummus due to the fact that it's simple to pair it with carrots for a fantastic treat. Or eat them by themselves.

38. Pineapple.

Pineapple is also tasty raw, however, barbecuing pineapple makes a currently mouthwatering fruit a lot more tasty.

39. Pomegranate seeds.

Sprinkle these extremely seeds on a salad, and you'll have yourself one sweet, tasty, and healthy meal.

40. Strawberries.

Eat a handful as a snack, or integrate these dazzling berries into your breakfast with this Easy Mint Yogurt with Strawberries recipe, and you will not be sorry.

41. Tofu.

Tofu is a vegetarian-friendly meat alternative because it's a complete protein. That's why you must include it to your Weight Watchers zero-point foods.

42. Turkey Breast.

Include this protein-packed food to the slow cooker, and you'll also have yourself a terrific addition to numerous meals throughout the week.

43. Lime.

Squeeze some fresh lime on dishes to perk things up. It's a great addition to a marinade.

44. Watermelon.

Much like its name implies, watermelon is packed with H2O. Given that it has a lot of water material, you should go ahead and get complete on it.

45. Greek Yogurt.

Get some plain, non-fat Greek yogurt.

46. Shrimp.

Protein-up with mouthwatering and sweet shrimp in this One-Pack Shrimp Bake. It's nearly simpler than any other technique, and it produces a very easy supper recipe.

47. Tilapia.

Given that fish is so helpful for you, you need to give your fish a delicious twist with a Parmesan Crusted Tilapia recipe.

48. Pumpkin.

Uncertain how to include pumpkin into your life? Start with the most crucial meal of the day.

49. Spinach.

This extremely low-calorie leafy green is a health maker. It looks like you must attempt it.

50. Calamari.

Skip the fried things and opt for Grilled Calamari. It's a seafood classic, and it's probably so much more delicious when made clean and healthy.

51. Tomatoes.

Since tomatoes are healthy and sweet, they're a choice for Weight Watchers zero-point foods you can make the most of.

52. Kiwi.

Firstly, this sweet, tropical fruit should already be on your mind.

53. Seaweed.

When you consider seaweed, you might think of sushi rolls. Comparable to sushi, consuming seaweed by itself, it can be a wonderful treat.

54. Tangerine.

First of all, tangerines will include some color to your meal. In addition, they will add tang to your meal. You ought to definitely attempt it.

55. Celery.

# WEIGHT WATCHERS SHOPPING LIST

Weight Watchers encourages members to keep weight-loss friendly foods on hand.

Getting healthy foods lessens temptation and makes sure that members have the components required to prepare fresh, yummy meals at home.

Here is a sample grocery list of Weight Watchers-approved foods.

Produce Fresh and frozen veggies and fruits, fresh herbs.

Protein: Lean meats, poultry, eggs, tofu, shellfish, frozen vegetable burgers and fish.

Dairy: Low-fat milk or nondairy milk replaces like almond milk, fat-free or low-fat unsweetened yogurt, fat-free home cheese, routine or low-fat cheeses.

Bread, pasta and grains: Brown rice, barley, quinoa, corn tortillas, whole-grain or reduced-calorie whole-grain, oatmeal and bread pasta, waffles or shredded cereal.

Canned and prepared foods: Tomato sauce, hummus, black bean dip, Weight Watchers frozen meals, salsa, canned beans, canned unsweetened fruits and canned low-salt vegetables.

Healthy fats: Olive oil, avocados, peanut butter, nuts and seeds.

Spices and condiments: Vinegar, hot sauce, mustard, dried herbs, fat-free mayo, reduced-sodium soy sauce, fat-free or low-fat salad dressing.

Snacks: Fat-free popcorn, baked tortilla chips, sugar-free gelatin, Weight Watchers ice cream bars and sorbet.

Weight Watchers motivates members to pick healthy choices when grocery shopping, including lean proteins, a lot of fresh and frozen fruits, veggies and whole grains.

## 3 WEEKS WEIGHT WATCHERS MEAL PLAN

After a busy day, it's good to be rewarded with a delicious evening meal-- however, a number of us merely don't have the energy or disposition to toil over complicated dishes to help meet our fitness goals.

But what if you could take a seat to a plate of succulent, sticky pork with noodles, or an aromatic Asian-style fish parcel, within half an hour of taking off your coat?

This isn't a pipeline dream, but the reality of today's tasty selection of weight watchers recipes, as they all take a maximum of 30 minutes to serve and prepare.

Planning is important to remain on track when hunger strikes-- and, with weight watchers' super-flexible method, the effort has actually already been done for you.

As laid out in this Saturday's Weekend magazine, weight watchers use the option of three plans-- Green, Blue and Purple-- so that you can select the one finest tailored to your lifestyle and consist of the foods you enjoy while still accomplishing the very same weight loss.

Not only is weight watchers packed full of fuss-free dishes; however, it likewise enables you to make your own easy-to-assemble meals from the ingredients you enjoy.

This is due to the fact that all three colour strategies are based on the scientifically proven WW SmartPoints system and include a plentiful list of ZeroPoint foods to take pleasure in without weighing or counting them towards your daily food spending plan.

Follow the plan that finest fits your life, and you might be on your method to losing up to half a stone quickly

Having a meal strategy is the very best way to remain on track with your weight-loss goals. We've made it easy by providing scrumptious ideas for breakfast, lunch, supper, and treats. Losing weight should not be a flavorless process! Healthy recipes that taste great is just among the factors that we enjoy this program. All you require are a few of the best dishes under your belt. Before you understand it, you'll drop severe pounds while enjoying your preferred foods.

You'll find whatever from tasty sausages to mouthwatering stews and muffins. Our 3 weeks Weight Watchers meal plan has all of it! Streamline your weight-loss journey by following a menu strategy that keeps meal stress at bay. For the next month, you do not need to stress over keeping yearnings in check. These nutrient-dense dishes are comforting and filling. So what are you waiting on? 3 weeks of tasty meals packed with nutrition and slimming residential or commercial properties start below.

Week 1

Day 1 (15 SmartPoints).

Breakfast: Individual Egg and Spinach Bowl Smart Points (Freestyle): 1.

Individual Egg & Spinach Bowls.

Protein:11 g.

Ingredients.

8 big egg whites (recommend free-range).

1 entire egg.

1 cup child spinach, torn or sliced into little pieces.

1/2 cup diced tomatoes.

1/4 cup feta cheese, fat-free.

1/2 teaspoon black pepper.

Kosher or sea salt to taste.

Guidelines.

Preheat oven to 350 degrees.

Blend together all active ingredients in a medium mixing bowl. Gently mist 4 (1/2 cup) ramekins with nonstick cooking spray and equally divide egg mixture into bowls.

Place ramekins on a cookie sheet and bake 20 minutes or until eggs puff and are practically set in the. Serve hot.

Lunch: Skinny Cheeseburger Boats SmartPoints (Freestyle): 5.

Skinny Cheeseburger Boats|Low-Calorie Burger Recipe.

Protein: 18g.

Active ingredients.

1 pound lean ground beef (optional ground turkey).

1 little onion, diced.

1/2 teaspoon sea salt.

1/2 teaspoon black pepper.

3 medium bell peppers of varied colors, (get rid of core, seeds, and membrane).

2/3 cup catsup, divided.

1 tablespoon mustard.

5 pieces (reduced-fat) cheddar cheese, (any cheese piece will work.

Guidelines.

Preheat oven to 375 degrees.

Slice each bell pepper into 6 vertical pieces, along the indention line. Set peppers aside.

In a big blending, bowl integrates meat, onion, salt, pepper, 1/3 cup ketchup, and mustard.

Add meat mix to boats. Put on a parchment lined baking sheet and cook until meat is done about 20 minutes.

Get rid of boats from the oven, drizzle with staying catsup, then top each with 1/4 cheese slice, place back in the oven and bake just till cheese is melted, about 5 minutes.

Enjoy and remove boats will hot!

Dinner: Crock Pot Low-Fat Beef Stew SmartPoints (Freestyle): 7.

Crock Pot Low-Fat Beef Stew.

Yields: 6 servings

1 pound lean beef stew meat, cubed in about 1-inch pieces.

2 tablespoons flour for finishing the beef.

1 cup red, white wine, (optional non-alcoholic white wine or vegetable broth).

1 teaspoon salt, divided.

1/2 teaspoon black pepper, divided.

2 tablespoons extra-virgin olive oil.

1 medium onion, coarsely chopped.

1 clove garlic, minced.

2 medium potatoes, peeled and cubed.

2 medium carrots, peeled and sliced.

2 celery stalks, coarsely sliced.

1/2 cup diced red peppers.

2 bay leaves.

6 sprigs of thyme, get rid of leaves from 4 sprigs.

2 cups beef fat-free, low-sodium and broth.

1 (14-ounce) can fire-roasted diced tomatoes.

Instructions.

Cover the beef with the flour then shake off the excess then sprinkle 1/2 teaspoon salt and 1/4 teaspoon black pepper.

Over medium heat, in a pan with extra-virgin olive oil, brown the floured beef then pour in the wine. Cook until sauce is somewhat thickened and alcohol aroma is gone about 5 minutes. Transfer the beef and its sauce to the crock pot.

In the crockery pot, include onion, garlic, potatoes, carrots, celery, red peppers, leaves from 4 thyme sprigs, bay leaves, broth, tomatoes, and the remaining 1/2 teaspoon salt and pepper. Cover and prepare on low for 8 hours or high 4 - 6 hours. Garnish with remaining two thyme sprigs.

Treat 3-Ingredient Parmesan Kale Chips SmartPoints (Freestyle): 2.

3-Ingredient Parmesan Kale Chips.

Yields: 6 servings

Active ingredients.

1 lot kale, coarsley and de-ribbed sliced.

1/2 cup freshly grated Parmesan cheese.

1 tablespoon extra-virgin olive oil.

Directions.

Preheat oven to 300 degrees.

Cut tough ribs and comes from kale. Chop leaves into large, bite-sized pieces.

Place chopped kale in a bowl. Add olive oil, tossing, and spray Parmesan to coat. Spread chips flat on a flat pan.

Bake for 15-20 minutes on the middle rack, up until browned and crisp in locations, stirring and rotating pan halfway through.

Take pleasure in!

Day 2 (17 SmartPoints).

Breakfast: Berry Overnight Oats SmartPoints (Freestyle): 5.

Berry Overnight Oats

Fiber: 7g

Ingredients.

1/2 cup rolled oats.

1/4 cup chia seeds.

1 cup of almond milk.

1/2 teaspoon vanilla extract.

2 tablespoons fresh blueberries.

2 tablespoons fresh raspberries.

2 teaspoons honey.

1/4 teaspoon cinnamon.

2 tablespoons shaved almonds.

Instructions.

Integrate all ingredients and blend well. Pour into an air tight container, cover, and cool over night. Serve cold with extra berries and almonds if desired.

IDEA: This recipe can be stored refrigerated for approximately one week in a covered air tight container.

Lunch: Slow Cooker Fiesta Chicken Soup SmartPoints (Freestyle): 1.

Slow Cooker Fiesta Chicken Soup.

Calories: 192

1/2 cup diced onion.

1 clove garlic, minced.

1 (15 oz.) can black beans, rinsed and drained.

1 (15 oz.) can kidney beans, rinsed and drained pipes.

1 (4.5 oz.) can dice green chili peppers.

1 (14.5 oz.) can diced tomatoes.

2 1/2 cups chicken broth, low salt, fat-free (use more broth for a thinner soup).

1 cup frozen or fresh corn.

Juice from 1 lime.

1 tablespoon chili powder.

1 teaspoon cumin.

1/2 teaspoon cayenne pepper (more or less to taste).

1/2 teaspoon black pepper.

Kosher or sea salt to taste.

1/2 cup freshly chopped cilantro.

2 chicken breasts fillets, skinless, cut into 1-2" cubes (no requirement to pre-cook).

Directions.

Add all components to the slow cooker, stir to combine — cover and cook on low 6-8 hours.

Supper: Sweet Potato Nachos SmartPoints (Freestyle): 5.

How to Make Sweet Potato Nachos Recipe.

Cholesterol: 29mg

Ingredients.

2 large sweet potatoes, cut into thin circles no greater than 1/4 inch thick.

1 tablespoon olive oil.

1/2 teaspoon Kosher salt.

1/2 cup skim milk.

1 cup fat-free shredded cheddar cheese.

1/4 cup black beans (cooked).

1/4 cup no-sugar included salsa.

1/4 cup jalapeno, sliced into thin strips.

1/4 cup tomato, diced small.

2 tablespoons red onion, diced small.

1 tablespoon fresh cilantro, sliced.

Directions.

Preheat oven to 400 degrees. Organize the sweet potatoes on a baking sheet in a single layer. Drizzle with olive oil and sprinkle with salt — Bake for 20 to 30 minutes or till golden brown and tender.

In a sauce pot, heat the milk blending continuously to prevent the milk from burning. When simmering, include the cheddar cheese and blend until thick and smooth. Get rid of from heat.

Get rid of the potatoes from the oven and let the potatoes cool somewhat before transferring to a serving plate. Set up the potatoes on a serving plate overlapping as necessary.

Snack: Sweet and Salty Chocolate Covered Pretzels SmartPoints (Freestyle): 6.

Sweet and Salty Chocolate Covered Pretzels.

Sugar: 8g

Ingredients.

1 (10 ounces) bag dark or semisweet chocolate chips (mini or routine are both fines).

1 (16 ounces) bag entire wheat mini pretzels, unsalted (if salted is just type offered, use those, however, do not garnish with sea salt).

2 teaspoons sea salt (flakes such as Maldon work well, but any kind of sea salt will do).

Instructions.

Line 2 baking sheets with wax paper.

Melt chocolate in a double boiler over medium heat on the stovetop.

To make your own double boiler, put a metal or heat-proof glass bowl or pot over a pot of one-inch simmering water. Simmering water ought to not touch the pot or bowl that is on top.

As soon as melted, get rid of from heat. Heat in safe microwave dish for 30-second intervals and get rid of each time to stir till melted.

Eliminate chocolate from heat.

Drop pretzels into melted chocolate a handful at a time. Eliminate one at a time with kitchen area tongs or a fork, shaking off excess chocolate back into the bowl and placing the pretzel on the wax paper. When each handful has actually been dipped in the chocolate and put on the wax paper, sprinkle with sea salt while still hot.

Operating in batches, finish all of the pretzels. Place the baking sheet in the fridge for a minimum of an hour for the chocolate to harden.

Day 3 (19 SmartPoints).

Breakfast: Instant Pot Apple Cinnamon Oatmeal SmartPoints (Freestyle): 2.

Instant Pot Apple Cinnamon Oatmeal.

Saturated Fat: 0 g

Active ingredients.

1 cup of steel cut oats.

2 1/2 cups water (3 cups for more loose oatmeal).

1 teaspoon ground cinnamon.

1 apple, peeled, core got rid of and chopped.

Honey to sweeten (optional).

Directions.

Include the oats, water, cinnamon, and apple to the Instant Pot and stir. Location the lid on the pot and guarantee the valve is sealed.

Press the Manual button and set to high pressure. Set the timer for 6 minutes. Once the pressure in the pot is attained, the timer will start, the Instant Pot will begin cooking and.

After the time is up, manually launch the steam and eliminate the lid. Stir and spoon into serving bowls. If using), drizzle with honey (. Serve hot and delight in!

Lunch: Mediterranean Chopped Salad with Salmon, Cucumber and Mint SmartPoints (Freestyle): 9.

Mediterranean Chopped Salad with Salmon, Cucumber and Mint.

Yields: 4 portions

Components.

2 cups romaine lettuce, approximately sliced.

2 big tomatoes, chopped little.

1 cucumber, chopped little.

1 yellow bell pepper, chopped small.

1/4 cup fresh parsley, sliced little.

2 tablespoons fresh mint, chopped small.

1 tablespoon lemon juice.

2 teaspoons lemon zest.

4 (6 ounces) salmon filets.

1/2 teaspoon kosher salt.

1/4 teaspoon ground black pepper.

Guidelines.

Preheat oven broiler to high or if a broiler is not readily available heat the over to 500 degrees.

In a large bowl, integrate the romaine, tomato, cucumber, bell pepper, parsley, mint, lemon juice, and 1 teaspoon of the lemon passion. Toss well and reserved.

Spray a baking sheet with nonstick spray and place the salmon filets on sheet. Sprinkle with salt and pepper. Location under the oven broiler can cook for about 10 minutes or until lightly browned on top and cooked through. Examine the half salmon way though and rotate the pan as needed so the salmon browns equally.

Spoon the salad into serving bowls and put the salmon on top. Sprinkle the remaining lemon passion on top of the salmon. Serve and enjoy!

Dinner: Baked Chicken Quesadilla Casserole SmartPoints (Freestyle): 6.

Baked Chicken Quesadilla Casserole.

Fiber: 6g

Active ingredients.

2 cups shredded and cooked chicken breast.

1/2 cup (fat-free) sour cream.

1 cup (reduced-fat) shredded cheddar cheese.

2 teaspoons ground cumin.

1 tablespoon chili powder.

1 teaspoon Kosher salt.

1/4 teaspoon ground black pepper.

1 cup corn kernels (canned or frozen, defrosted).

1 (15 ounces) can black beans, drained and washed.

4 larger entire grain tortillas, a recipe for tortillas.

Directions.

Pre-heat the oven o 400 degrees. Spray a 9 x 13 inch casserole dish with non stick spray.

In a large bowl, combine the chicken, sour cream, half the cheese, half the cumin, half the chili powder, salt, and half the pepper. Mix well.

In a second bowl, combine the corn, black beans, the staying cumin, chili powder, and pepper. Mix well.

Lay two of the tortillas in the bottom of the casserole meal. Spread half of the chicken mix over the tortillas and half the bean mix over the chicken. Place the staying tortillas over the beans and repeat. Sprinkle the staying cheese on top.

Bake for 20 to 30 minutes or up until cheese is melted. Serve hot.

Snack: Oven-Baked Zucchini Chips SmartPoints (Freestyle): 2.

Oven Baked Zucchini Chips.

Calories: 99

1 (large) zucchini, cut into 1/8" - 1/4" pieces.

1/3 cup entire grain breadcrumbs, optional Panko (homemade breadcrumb dish).

1/4 cup finely grated parmesan cheese, lowered fat.

1/4 teaspoon black pepper.

Kosher or sea salt to taste.

1/8 teaspoon garlic powder.

1/8 teaspoon cayenne pepper.

3 tablespoons low-fat milk.

Instructions.

Preheat oven to 425 degrees.

Combine in a small blending bowl, breadcrumbs, parmesan cheese, black pepper, salt, garlic powder, and cayenne pepper. Dip zucchini slices into milk and dig up into bread crumbs to coat both sides. Keep in mind: It may be essential to press crumbs onto zucchini slices to make sure the crumbs stick.

Set up zucchini on a non-stick cookie sheet and lightly mist with a non-stick cooking spray.

Location rack on a cookie sheet if using a rack. Bake 15 minutes, turn over and continue baking till golden, roughly 10-15 minutes (bewaring not to burn). Permit to cool to room temperature level before storing in an airtight container.

SUGGESTION: Zucchini Chips will continue to get crispier while cooling.

KEEP IN MIND: For gluten free chips, use gluten-free bread crumbs.

Day 4 (18 SmartPoints).

Breakfast: Turkey Sausage Breakfast Muffins SmartPoints (Freestyle): 5.

Turkey Sausage Breakfast Muffins.

Cholesterol: 60mg

Components.

1/2 pound turkey sausage.

1/4 cup green bell pepper, diced.

1/4 cup red onion, diced.

3 cups entire wheat bread, diced into 1/2 inch cubes.

2 cup low fat shredded cheddar cheese.

6 egg whites.

2 eggs.

1/4 cup skim milk.

1/2 teaspoon Kosher salt.

Guidelines.

Preheat oven to 350 degrees. Line muffin tin with 12 paper muffin cup liners or lightly spray with non stick spray.

In a medium frying pan, cook turkey sausage, separating into small pieces as it cooks. Prepare until no pink remains. Include green pepper and onion to the sausage and cook up until soft.

Divide bread cubes between 12 muffin cups. Spoon turkey sausage mix on top of bread crumbs and cheese on top of the turkey mix. Just fill cups about 3/4 complete.

In a bowl, blend together egg whites, eggs, milk, and salt. Put over bread, sausage, and cheese filled muffin cups. Just fill to just cover the ingredients in the muffin cups. If required, permit to rest for 5 minutes and add more egg mix to the cups.

Bake for 15 to 20 minutes till embeded in the middle and tops begin to brown. Enable to rest for 5 minutes before getting rid of from muffin tin. Serve warm.

Lunch: Moroccan Chicken Salad with Chimichurri Dressing SmartPoints (Freestyle): 6.

Moroccan Chicken Salad with Chimichurri Dressing.

Overall Fat: 19g

Active ingredients.

For the Chimichurri Dressing:

1 clove garlic.

1 cup of fresh cilantro.

1/4 cup fresh parsley.

1 tablespoon lemon juice.

3 tablespoons olive oil.

1/4 teaspoon Kosher salt.

Pinch of crushed red pepper.

For the Salad:

1 1/2 cups skinless and boneless chicken breast, cooked and shredded (leftovers work terrific).

6 cups child arugula.

1 cup of shredded carrot.

1 cup cucumber, chopped.

1/4 cup pomegranate seeds.

1/4 cup fat free feta cheese crumbles.

1/4 cup chopped almonds.

Guidelines.

For the Chimichurri Dressing:

Integrate all components in a food processor and pulse until carefully chopped and well mixed. Set aside.

For the Salad:

Combine all ingredients in a large bowl and toss. Divide into serving bowls and drizzle about 1 to 2 tablespoons of Chimichurri Dressing over the top. Serve and enjoy.

Supper: Clean Eating Pizza Lasagna Rolls SmartPoints (Freestyle): 7.

Pizza Lasagna Rolls.

Trans Fat: 0 g

Sauce (optional: usage 1 (24-ounce) jar marinara instead of homemade sauce).

2 cloves garlic, minced.

1 tablespoon extra-virgin olive oil.

2 (14-ounce) cans diced tomatoes with liquid.

1 1/4 teaspoons dried oregano.

1/2 teaspoon kosher or sea.

1/4 teaspoon black pepper.

Lasagna.

1/2 cup parmesan cheese, grated.

2 cups shredded part-skim mozzarella.

1/2 cup ricotta cheese.

1/4 teaspoon pepper.

1 teaspoon dried oregano.

10 whole grain lasagna noodles, boiled according to plan.

Guidelines.

Over medium heat, in a pan with extra-virgin olive oil, sautè the garlic for 1 minute. Include the canned tomatoes, bring to a boil then lower the heat to a simmer. Season with salt, pepper, and dried oregano then simmer for 15 - 10 minutes.

Pre-heat the oven to 375 degrees F.

Pour 1 cup sauce in the bottom of a 13 x 9-inch casserole pan, reserved.

Combine cheeses, pepper, and oregano. Evenly spread out cheese mixture over each lasagna roll, retaining 1/2 cup for the top. Drizzle 1 tablespoon sauce over cheese roll to close, then place on the baking dish, seam side down.

Put 1 1/2 cups sauce over the top and spray on remaining cheese mixture. Serve any remaining sauce with rolls. Loosely cover with foil and bake in the preheated oven for 25-30 minutes or up until cheese is totally melted.

Let the rolls rest for a few minutes prior to serving.

Snack: Baked Apple Chips SmartPoints (Freestyle): 0.

Baked Apple Chips.

Cholesterol: 0 mg

2 apples, cored and very finely sliced.

Cinnamon to taste.

Directions.

Preheat oven to 275 degrees.

Line a cookie sheet with parchment paper and place the pieces of chopped apple on top.

Sprinkle with cinnamon (to taste).

Bake at 275 degrees for 2 hours. After 60 minutes, turn them over, so they bake uniformly. Because oven cook times vary and you don't want to burn them, you must inspect on them after 60 minutes and every 30 minutes after that. Once they look crispy and great remove them from the oven and allow to cool.

Day 5 (17 SmartPoints).

Breakfast: Souffle Omelette with Mushrooms SmartPoints (Freestyle): 1.

Souffle Omelette with Mushrooms.

Carbohydrates: 2 g

Active ingredients.

1 teaspoon extra-virgin olive oil.

1 clove garlic, minced.

8 ounces sliced mushrooms.

1 tablespoon parsley, minced.

3 big eggs, separated.

1/2 teaspoon salt.

1/2 teaspoon pepper.

1/4 cup grated cheese.

Guidelines.

Over medium heat, in a skillet, warm olive oil and sautè the garlic.

Include the mushrooms and sautè for 10 minutes. Include the parsley then shut off the heat. Reserve.

(We utilized a blender for the egg whites). Fold the whites into the yolks, including cheese, and salt and pepper.

Spray a large skillet with nonstick spray.

Put in the egg mixture then cover. Prepare up until the top and bottom are set.

With the help of a spatula, loosen it carefully. Include the mushrooms to the omelette then carefully fold over. Serve hot.

Lunch: Tuna Salad Stuffed Avocado SmartPoints (Freestyle): 8.

Tuna Salad Stuffed Avocado.

Salt: 536mg

Ingredients.

1/2 tablespoon olive oil.

6 ounce fresh tuna filet (such as ahi or blue fin tuna) * See choice for canned tuna below.

2 tablespoons plain Greek yogurt, optioal Clean Mayo.

1 tablespoon lemon juice.

2 tablespoons red onion, minced.

1 tablespoon celery, minced.

1/4 cup cucumber, diced small.

1 teaspoon garlic powder.

1/4 teaspoon cayenne pepper.

1/2 teaspoon Kosher salt.

1/2 teaspoon dry dill.

1 entire avocado.

Instructions.

Heat olive oil in a frying pan on medium heat. Once hot, add tuna filet and sear on each side to a golden brown.

When cool, diced tuna into a small cube. Include remaining ingredients, other than avocado, and gently toss. Set aside.

OPTION: 2 (5 ounces) cans of tuna may be replacement for fresh tuna. Do not scorch canned tuna, mix into other components as directed. We recommend Safe Catch brand name.

Leaving the peel on the avocado, halved, getting rid of the pit. If required, carefully cut a "dent" into the center of each half to develop a bowl.

Divide tuna salad between each half, placing in the center of the avocado bowl. Enjoy and serve!

Supper: Turkey Meatloaf Cupcakes with Mashed Potatoes SmartPoints (Freestyle): 6.

Turkey Meatloaf Cupcakes with Mashed Potatoes.

Fiber: 3g

Ingredients.

Meatloaf.

1 pound lean ground turkey breast.

1 egg, beaten.

1/2 cup whole wheat breadcrumbs.

1/4 cup ketchup.

1/2 cup diced onion.

1/2 cup grated carrots (grate on large holes of a cheese/box grater).

1/2 cup carefully sliced fresh parsley leaves.

1 clove garlic, minced, or 1 teaspoon garlic powder.

2 teaspoons Worcestershire sauce.

1/2 teaspoon kosher or sea salt.

1/2 teaspoon black pepper.

1 teaspoon dried oregano.

Mash.

2 big russet potatoes, peeled and chopped.

1 tablespoon extra virgin olive oil or butter.

1/2 cup low-fat milk.

1/4 teaspoon kosher or sea salt.

Guidelines.

Preheat oven to 350 degrees. Spray 12 cups of a muffin tin kindly with cooking spray.

Location potatoes in a pot of cold salted water over high heat and bring to a boil. Reduce heat to medium-high. Cook until tender when pierced with a fork, about 20 minutes. Drain pipes. Mash potatoes with olive oil, salt, and milk.

Meanwhile, mix meatloaf components in a large bowl. Hands may be used. Divide meatloaf evenly into 12 muffin cups, 3/4 of the way full, pressing the meat in.

Bake for 35 minutes. The inside must read 165 degrees when pierced with a meat thermometer. Cool muffins for about 4 to 5 minutes, eliminate from the tin, and spread each uniformly with mashed potatoes, raising spatula to develop peaks if preferred.

Delight in!


Snack: Southwestern Brussels Sprout Coleslaw SmartPoints (Freestyle): 2.

Southwestern Brussels Sprout Coleslaw.

Protein: 4g.

Ingredients.

4 cups Brussels sprouts, shaved or carefully sliced.

1 cup kale, approximately chopped.

3 tablespoons red onion, finely minced.

1/2 cup charred corn kernels.

1 tablespoon jalapeno, minced.

1/4 cup tomatoes, diced little.

1/4 cup lime juice.

1 cup avocado, mashed.

2 teaspoons honey.

1/2 teaspoon kosher salt.

1 teaspoon ground cuming.

1 table spoon chili powder.

Instructions.

In a large blending bowl, combine the Brussels sprouts, kale, corn, onion, jalapeno, and tomatoes. Gently toss.

In a small blending bowl, integrate the remaining ingredients to make a sauce. Contribute to the Brussels sprouts mix and toss until everything is covered in the avocado sauce. Cool for a minimum of 30 minutes prior to serving. Delight in!

Day 6 (16 SmartPoints).

Breakfast: Peanut Butter Banana Overnight Oats SmartPoints (Freestyle): 7.

Peanut Butter Banana Overnight Oats.

Yield: about 2 cups

Ingredients.

1/2 cup rolled oats.

1 cup of almond milk.

1 tablespoon chia seeds.

1/4 teaspoon vanilla extract.

1/2 teaspoon ground cinnamon.

1 tablespoon honey, (maple syrup for a vegan option).

1 banana, sliced.

2 tablespoons natural creamy peanut butter.

Guidelines.

Integrate the oats, milk, chila seeds, vanilla, cinnamon, and honey. Mix well. Pour a percentage into 2 glass jars or other serving containers.

Layer the banana and peanut butter and put the remaining oat mixture over the top. Cover, seal and let sit overnight. Serve cooled.

Lunch: Tomato, Mozzarella, and Basil Panini SmartPoints (Freestyle): 8.

Tomato, Mozzarella, and Basil Panini.

Carbohydrates: 15g

Components.

2 slices entire wheat bread.

1/2 cup shredded part-skim mozzarella.

1 Roma tomato, very finely sliced.

1 thin piece of red onion.

8 fresh basil leaves.

Pinch of kosher or sea salt.

1/8 teaspoon pepper.

1 tablespoon extra-virgin olive oil.

Directions.

Spread olive oil with a pastry or basting brush over 2 slices of bread. Spray each with salt and pepper.

Place one of the bread slices, oil-side down and top basil leaves, tomato pieces, onion, and mozzarella. Leading with other pieces of bread, olive oil side up.

Place a heavy-bottomed frying pan on the stovetop over medium-high heat or utilize a Panini press.

If utilizing a frying pan, press down with lid to flatten sandwich a bit. Prepare for about 2 minutes, until golden on the bottom, and flip. Repeat on the opposite.

Slice sandwich in half to make 2 portions.

Delight in!

Dinner: Slow Cooker Balsamic Chicken SmartPoints (Freestyle): 1.

Slow Cooker Balsamic Chicken.

Protein 25 g

Active ingredients.

4-6 boneless, skinless, chicken breasts (about 40 ounces).

2 14.5 oz can diced tomatoes.

1 medium onion thinly sliced (Not chopped).

4 garlic cloves.

1/2 cup balsamic vinegar (for gluten-free usage White Balsamic Vinegar which does not have caramel coloring).

1 tablespoon olive oil.

1 teaspoon dried oregano.

1 teaspoon dried basil.

1 teaspoon dried rosemary.

1/2 teaspoon thyme.

ground black pepper and salt to taste.

Instructions.

Pour the olive oil on the bottom of the slow cooker, including chicken breasts, salt and pepper each breast, put the chopped onion on top of chicken then put in all the dried herbs and garlic cloves. Gather vinegar and top with tomatoes.

Prepare on high 4 hours, serve over angel hair pasta.


Snack: Instant Pot Applesauce SmartPoints (Freestyle): 0.

instant Pot Applesauce.

Calories: 177

Ingredients.

6 to 8 medium apples (we advise a combination of Granny Smith and Gala apples.

1 cup of water.

1 teaspoon lemon juice.

2 teaspoons cinnamon (optional).

Guidelines.

Peel and cut apples into 2 inch pieces — location apples and all other active ingredients into the Instant Pot.

Close Instant Pot cover, guaranteeing the vent remains in the sealed position. Press the "manual" button and get used to high pressure and set the timer to 8 minutes. The Instant Pot will preheat before starting the cooking time.

As soon as the timer goes off, let sit for about 2-3 minutes. Turn the steam vent to release pressure and thoroughly remove and release the steam lid.

Drain pipes off any excess water. Location cooked apples in a mixture and mix on low up until preferred applesauce consistency is reached - smooth or chunky! Allow cooling somewhat before serving.

KEEP IN MIND: This recipe can also be used when canning or freezing applesauce!

Day 7 (21 SmartPoints).

Breakfast: Peanut Butter Mocha Espresso Shake SmartPoints (Freestyle): 11.

Peanut Butter Mocha Espresso Shake.

Cholesterol: 0 mg

Active ingredients.

1/2 frozen banana.

1 tablespoon peanut butter.

1 tablespoon unsweetened cocoa powder.

1/2 cup almond milk.

1/2 cup strong brewed coffee, cooled.

3/4 cup ice.

Instructions.

Combine all ingredients in a mixer. Mix until smooth.

Lunch: Skinny Taco Salad in a Jar SmartPoints (Freestyle): 3.

Skinny Taco Salad in a Jar.

Sugars: 3 g

Salad:

1/2 pound ground turkey.

1 teaspoon chili powder.

1/2 teaspoon cumin.

1/4 teaspoon garlic powder.

1/4 teaspoon sea salt.

1/2 cup whole grain tortilla chips, broken.

1/2 cup shredded cheddar cheese, reduced-fat.

3 cups sliced romaine lettuce.

1 cup cut in half cherry tomatoes.

1/2 cup salsa, no sugar added.

Velvety Salsa Dressing: (optional).

2 tablespoons plain Greek yogurt.

2 tablespoons ripe, mashed avocado.

Juice of 1 lime.

1/4 cup salsa.

Instructions.

Heat a frying pan over medium heat and include the turkey. Cook till turkey is no longer pink and cooked through. Add spices, stir to integrate and transfer to a bowl and let cool.

To make the salad, divide the tortilla chips between six jars. Layer each with the salsa, turkey mix, tomatoes, lettuce, and cheese.

Make the optional dressing by mixing the yogurt, avocado, lime juice, and salsa in a mixer. Top the salad with the dressing, seal the containers and store in the fridge up until ready to consume.

Supper: Skinny Zucchini Pasta & Baby Spinach SmartPoints (Freestyle): 4.

Skinny Zucchini Pasta & Baby Spinach.

Sugar: 5g

Components.

4 medium zucchini, peeled and ends gotten rid of.

1 teaspoon kosher or sea salt.

2 tablespoons extra-virgin olive oil.

3 cloves garlic, minced.

1 (15 ounces) can diced tomatoes.

1 tablespoon capers.

1/4 cup Italian parsley.

1 1/2 teaspoons dried oregano.

1/2 teaspoon black pepper.

1/4 teaspoon crushed red pepper flakes.

1 cup loosely loaded infant spinach.

1/2 cup freshly grated parmesan cheese.

Directions.

Location each zucchini on a veggie spiralizer to make the pasta. Utilize the smaller sized holes for spaghetti.

Optional: Sprinkle 1/2 teaspoon salt on zucchini pasta, tossing to coat. Spread pasta on double layer of paper towels on a flat pan, which will draw out a few of the water. Allow setting for 10 minutes.

Add olive oil to a large frying pan over medium-low heat.

Include garlic and sauté for 1 minute.

Raise heat to medium, add tomatoes with liquid, capers, parsley, oregano, black pepper, red pepper, staying salt, and zucchini pasta, tossing to combine.

Prepare until pasta is tender, about 7-8 minutes.

Add spinach and prepare just up until wilted, about 1 minute.

Contribute to a serving platter and spray with parmesan.

Delight in!


Snack: Baked Onion Rings SmartPoints (Freestyle): 3.

Baked Onion Rings.

Serving Size: 1/4 of dish

1 big sweet or red onion, very finely sliced into rings.

1/2 cup gluten-free Panko, or entire grain bread crumbs (bread crumb recipe).

1/2 cup flour, optional gluten totally free flour.

1/2 teaspoon baking power.

1/4 teaspoon black pepper.

Kosher or sea salt to taste.

1 egg white.

3/4 cup low-fat milk or low-fat buttermilk.

Guidelines.

Preheat oven to 400 degrees.

In a medium blending, combine panko or whole wheat bread crumbs, flour, salt, pepper and baking powder. Different the onion pieces into private rings and contribute to the flour mix, carefully toss and make certain all the rings are covered. Remove onions and reserved.

Blend together milk and egg white, add to the remaining flour mix and stir to combine. Flip onion rings after 10 minutes.

Keep in mind: If utilizing this recipe for Green Bean Casserole, lower cooking time by 5 minutes as the onion rings will continue to brown while on top of the casserole.

Week 2

Day 8 (16 SmartPoints).

Breakfast: Rise and Shine With These Greek Egg Muffins SmartPoints (Freestyle): 1.

Rise and Shine With These Greek Egg Muffins!

Salt: 155mg

Ingredients.

2 eggs.

4 egg whites.

1/2 cup skim milk.

1/2 teaspoon Kosher salt.

1/4 teaspoon ground white pepper.

1/4 cup tomatoes, diced little.

1/4 cup red onion, diced little.

1/4 cup black olives, diced little.

1 tablespoon fresh parsley, approximately sliced.

1/4 cup fat totally free feta cheese, collapsed, (optional).

Directions.

Preheat oven to 350 and spray a 6 count muffin tin with non-stick spray.

In a mixing bowl, integrate the eggs, pepper, milk and salt. Blend well up until somewhat frothy. Stir in staying components.

Fill muffin tin with the egg mix, filling each muffin cup about 3/4 complete. Bake for 15-20 minutes or till the egg muffins have cooked through and lightly browned on top. Serve instantly or shop and reheat for a fast grab and go breakfast!

Lunch: Clean Eating Chicken Salad SmartPoints (Freestyle): 2.

Clean Eating Chicken Salad.

Protein: 25 g.

Ingredients.

2 prepared skinless, boneless chicken breasts - cut into cubes.

2 celery stalks, sliced.

1/4 red onion, sliced.

1/2 cup red seedless grapes, quartered.

1/2 cup Greek yogurt, non-fat.

1 tsp garlic powder.

1 tsp newly ground black pepper.

Sea salt to taste.

2 whole-wheat pita pockets, cut in half.

4 romaine lettuce leaves.

Instructions.

In a big bowl, blend all of the salad ingredients. Chicken salad can be eaten as is or consume as a pita sandwich. Recipe serves 4.

Supper: 6-Ingredient Mexican Style Quinoa Salad SmartPoints (Freestyle): 5.

6-Ingredient Mexican-Style Quinoa Salad.

Protein: 13 g.

Ingredients

1/2 cup dry quinoa, pre-rinsed.

1 (15-ounce) can black beans, drained pipes and washed.

1 cups salsa, no-sugar added.

1 cup of corn kernels.

1 teaspoon chili powder.

1 avocado, peeled and small diced.

Directions.

Include 1 cup water and quinoa to a medium pot and give a rolling boil over medium-high heat. Reduce heat to a simmer, cover and cook up until the majority of moisture is absorbed, about 12-15 minutes. Switch off the heat and leave covered quinoa on the burner for 5 minutes.

Contribute to prepared quinoa, black beans, chili, corn, and salsa powder. Include salt and pepper to taste. Toss to combine then include diced avocado and gently toss. Add a salad to a serving meal and serve. Salad can also be taken pleasure in the cold.

Snack: Coconut Banana Paleo Cookies SmartPoints (Freestyle): 8.

Coconut Banana Paleo Cookies.

Salt: 148mg

Components.

3 cups almond flour.

1 teaspoon baking soda.

1/2 teaspoon kosher or sea salt.

1 teaspoon cinnamon.

1/4 cup (grass-fed) unsalted butter, space temperature level, (optional coconut oil).

3/4 cup coconut sugar.

1 big egg, beaten.

1 large egg white.

1 teaspoon pure vanilla.

1 overly ripe banana (1/2 cup), mashed.

1 cup finely shredded coconut, unsweetened.

1 cup walnut pieces.

Directions.

Blend together in a medium bowl, almond flour, baking soda, salt, and cinnamon. Add walnuts and coconut, and stir into the flour mix.

In a medium blending bowl, utilizing a beater, cream together butter and coconut sugar. Add egg, egg white, and vanilla, mixing until combined. Stir in mashed banana and coconut, till integrated.

Add flour mixture to damp ingredients and simply stir. Cover and refrigerate 45 minutes.

Preheat oven to 350 degrees.

Using a 1-1/2 inch cookie or ice cream scoop, drop dough 2-inches apart on a big, parchment lined, cookie sheet. Bake 8 minutes and turn cookie sheet. Bake an extra 8 minutes, or until golden and just set. Enable cookies to cool 5 minutes while still on the cookie sheet. Move cookies to a cake rack and cool totally. Continue baking cookies till all dough is used.

Shop in an airtight container as much as two days. Include 1 cup Paleo friendly chocolate chips when adding the walnuts if preferred.

Day 9 (11 SmartPoints).

Breakfast: Crustless Vegetable Quiche SmartPoints (Freestyle): 2.

Crustless Vegetable Quiche Recipe.

Protein: 11 g.

Ingredients.

1 tablespoon olive oil.

1 little yellow onion, diced.

2 cloves garlic, mined.

1/2 cup diced red bell pepper.

1/2 cup diced green bell pepper.

1/2 cup sliced zucchini.

6 broccoli florets.

1/4 cup diced sun-dried tomatoes.

3 big eggs.

4 big egg whites.

2 tablespoons low-fat milk.

1 teaspoon dried oregano.

1/2 teaspoon black pepper.

Sea Salt to taste.

1/4 cup plus 1 tablespoon low-fat parmesan cheese, optional.

Guidelines.

Preheat oven to 425 degrees.

In a large frying pan on medium-low heat, add oil and sauté onion and garlic until tender, about 4 minutes. Include diced bell pepper, zucchini, broccoli and sun-dried tomatoes and continue sautéing 2 minutes.

In a medium mixing bowl, blend together eggs, egg whites, milk, spices and 1/4 cup parmesan cheese. Gently spray a 9" pie dish, add sautéed veggies. Pour egg mix over vegetables, ensure to cover all veggies.

Loosely cover with foil and bake 10 minutes at 425 degrees, decrease the heat to 350 and continue baking 20-25 minutes. Remove foil the last couple of minutes of baking time and sprinkle with the staying parmesan cheese. Quiche is done when it puffs, and a knife placed in the center comes out clean.

Lunch: Tomato, Hummus, and Spinach Sandwich SmartPoints (Freestyle): 3.

Tomato, Hummus, and Spinach Sandwich.

Salt: 308 mg

2 slices multigrain bread.

2 tablespoons roasted garlic hummus or hummus of choice.

3 pieces tomato.

1/2 cup infant spinach.

1/8 teaspoon salt (a pinch sprinkled on).

Instructions.

Toast multigrain bread (if desired). Spread hummus on top of one slice of bread. Top with tomato slices and layer with spinach. Spinkle on the salt place the second piece of bread on top enjoy and serve!

Supper: Slow Cooker Spinach Artichoke Chicken SmartPoints (Freestyle): 5.

Slow Cooker Spinach Artichoke Chicken.

Serving Size: 1 chicken breast and 1/4 of the spinach, tomatoes, and artichokes

8 cups loosely loaded spinach, chopped.

1 cup of chicken broth.

4 (6-8 ounce) entire chicken breasts (bone-in with skin).

3 cloves fresh garlic, chopped.

1/4 sweet onion, finely chopped.

4 tablespoons cream cheese, reduced-fat but not fat totally free.

4 tablespoons shredded parmesan cheese.

1 (14-ounce) can preservative-free artichoke hearts OR 6-8 artichoke hearts from a container, drained pipes and sliced.

1 cup chopped grape or cherry tomatoes.

salt and pepper to taste.

Guidelines.

Place spinach, chicken broth, and chicken breasts in a 4-quart slow cooker. Sprinkle with onion, salt, and garlic and pepper — Cook and cover on low for 6-8 hours, or on high from 4-6 hours.

Just prior to serving, carefully remove chicken breasts from the slow cooker and location on serving plates — spoon sauce over chicken.

Top with tomatoes. Sprinkle with extra parmesan cheese, if wanted.

Treat Paleo Friendly Meaty Veggie Roll Ups SmartPoints (Freestyle): 1.

Meaty Veggie Roll-Ups.

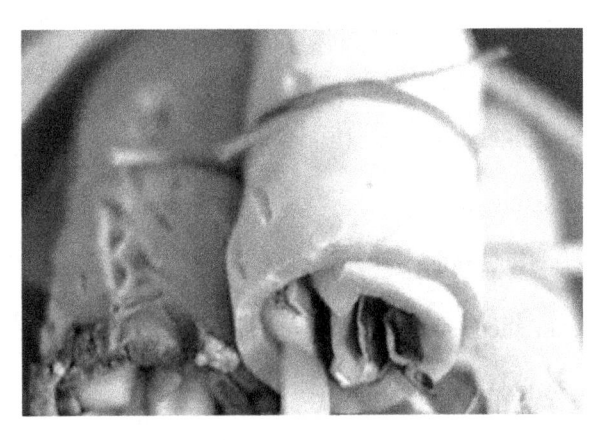

Cholesterol: 29 mg

12 thick slices unprocessed deli meat, we recommend Boar's Head Brand.

1 cup of sliced vegetables.

12 chives, optional.

Instructions.

Place wanted amount of vegetables on a piece of deli meat. Roll securely, and if preferred, utilize a chive to tie — Cram in a zip-top plastic bag or airtight container.

Preferred Flavor Combinations:

Roast beef with red bell pepper strips, carrot sticks, and cucumber pieces with mustard for dipping.

Chicken with apple slices, red cabbage, and pickle strips with Dijon mustard for dipping.

Turkey with crumbled bacon and chopped avocado with salsa for dipping.

Day 10 (24 SmartPoints).

Breakfast: Overnight French Toast Casserole SmartPoints (Freestyle): 6.

Overnight French Toast Casserole.

Salt: 433 mg

1 (13 ounces) loaf whole wheat French bread, sliced into 20 pieces.

8 big eggs.

2 cups low-fat milk, optional almond milk.

1 teaspoon pure vanilla extract.

1 teaspoon cinnamon.

2 tablespoons coconut palm sugar or honey.

Topping.

1/4 cup sucanat, optional coconut palm sugar or honey.

1/2 cup minced pecans.

1 teaspoon cinnamon.

Directions.

Gently mist a 9" x 13" x 2" casserole meal with non-stick cooking spray. Set up bread pieces in 2 rows, slightly overlapping pieces. In a large mixing bowl, blend together eggs, milk, vanilla, cinnamon and sucanat. Pour mix over the bread, making certain all bread is moist. Cover and cool overnight.

Preheat oven to 350 degrees. Integrate topping components, sprinkle equally over the top of bread and bake 35 to 40 minutes, or up until golden. Serve with fresh berries or a drizzle of pure maple syrup.

KEEP IN MIND: Whole Wheat French Bread can be acquired in the pastry shop section at a lot of Walmart Super Centers, for about $1.00.

Lunch: Supermodel Superfood Salad SmartPoints (Freestyle): 6.

Supermodel Superfood Salad.

Carbohydrates: 12 g

One head of kale.

1/4 cup pine nuts.

1/2 cup dried cranberries or currants.

Juice of 1 lemon.

1/4 cup extra-virgin olive oil.

Pinch of sea salt.

Instructions.

Remove and dispose of big stems of kale leaves. Coarsely chop kale leaves and include to a big serving bowl. Include pine nuts, dried cranberries or currants.

Squeeze the juice of one lemon, drizzle with olive oil, and sprinkle salt, toss to combine.

If desired, garnish with 1/4 cup freshly grated parmesan cheese.

Supper: Asian Mango Chicken Stir-Fry SmartPoints (Freestyle): 8.

Asian Mango Chicken Stir-Fry.

Yields: 5 servings

Ingredients.

1 tablespoon olive oil.

4 boneless, skinless chicken breasts, sliced.

1 little onion, sliced.

1 red pepper, sliced.

1 green pepper, sliced.

2 mangos, peeled and sliced.

1 teaspoon ground ginger.

2 tablespoons low salt chicken stock.

2 tablespoons soy sauce.

2 tablespoons of rice vinegar.

1 tablespoon pulp-free orange juice.

2 tablespoons cornstarch.

1 teaspoon black pepper.

1/2 teaspoon kosher salt.

Guidelines.

Heat the oil over medium heat in a pan. Add the chicken and saute for 4 minutes. Get rid of chicken from the pan and add the onion. Cook until translucent, then add peppers. Prepare 3 minutes then return the chicken. In a little bowl, blend together the staying components and put over the stir fry.

Cook for 8 minutes, then serve over rice.

Snack: Skinny Bell Pepper Nacho Boats SmartPoints (Freestyle): 4.

Skinny Bell Pepper Nacho Boats.

Trans Fat: 0g

Active ingredients.

1 pound lean ground turkey.

1 teaspoon chili powder.

1 teaspoon cumin.

1/2 teaspoon black pepper.

1/4 teaspoon kosher or sea salt.

3/4 cup salsa, no sugar included.

1 cup grated cheddar cheese, reduced-fat.

3 bell peppers.

Directions.

Eliminate seeds, core, and membrane from bell peppers then slice every one into 6 verticle pieces where they dip down. Set sliced bell peppers aside.

Cook ground turkey over medium-high heat, separating as it cooks. Cook up until the turkey loses it's a pink color and is cooked through. Drain pipes off any fat.

Preheat oven to 375 degrees.

Combine prepared turkey with spices and salsa. Equally distribute mixture into the bell pepper boats, top with cheese.

Bake on a parchment lined baking sheet for 10 minutes or till cheese is melted and peppers are hot. Optional ingredients: sliced Jalepeno peppers, diced avocado, fat-free Greek yogurt or sour cream, or sliced up green onions.

NOTE: If you choose much softer bell peppers, add a couple of tablespoons water to the bottom of a large casserole dish, include filled nachos, cover securely with foil and bake 15 minutes.

Day 11 (20 SmartPoints).

Breakfast: Flour-less Blueberry Oatmeal Muffins SmartPoints (Freestyle): 5.

Flour-less Blueberry Oatmeal Muffins.

Cholesterol: 16mg

Ingredients.

2 1/2 cups old-fashioned rolled oats.

1 1/2 cups almond milk.

1 large egg, lightly beaten.

1/3 cup pure maple syrup.

2 tablespoons melted coconut oil.

1 teaspoon vanilla extract.

1 teaspoon ground cinnamon.

1 teaspoon baking powder.

1/4 teaspoon salt.

1 teaspoon grated lemon zest.

1 cup of fresh blueberries.

Directions.

Integrate the oats and almond milk in a large mixing bowl. Cover and refrigerate over night.

Preheat oven to 375 degrees. Spray a muffin tin with non-stick spray or line with muffin pan liners.

Carefully stir all components into the soaked oats mixture. Spoon into the prepared muffin pan, filling about 3/4 full.

Bake for about 20 minutes or up until tops is golden. Serve warm.

Lunch: Chicken and Crisp Veggie Sandwich SmartPoints (Freestyle): 8.

Chicken and Crisp Veggie Sandwich.

Carbohydrates: 41 g

2 pieces whole wheat or whole grain bread, toasted if wanted.

1 cooked (3 oz) boneless, skinless chicken breast.

1 radish, thinly sliced.

4- 5 slices cucumber.

2 thin slices red onion (optional).

1 lettuce leaf, cut in half.

1 tablespoon guacamole, hummus, or spread of option.

Directions.

Assemble each sandwich by adding 1 tablespoon infect each slice of bread, then topped with radish, cucumber, romaine lettuce and chicken breasts. Leading with extra piece bread, turn over, cut in half, and serve.

Dinner: Baked Lemon Salmon and Asparagus Foil Pack SmartPoints (Freestyle): 2.

Baked Lemon Salmon and Asparagus Foil Pack.

Protein: 32g.

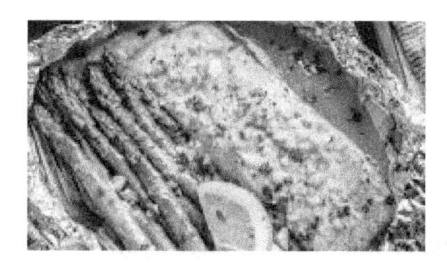

Active ingredients.

4 (4 to 6 ounce) filets salmon.

1 pound fresh asparagus, about 1 inch of the bottom ends cut off.

1 teaspoon Kosher salt.

1/2 teaspoon ground black pepper.

2 tablespoons olive oil.

1/4 cup fresh lemon juice.

1 tablespoon fresh thyme, chopped.

2 tablespoons fresh parsley, chopped.

2 tablespoons lemon passion.

Instructions.

Pre-heat the oven to 400 degrees.

Lay 4 big sheets of foil on a flat surface and spray with nonstick spray. Divide the asparagus in between each of the packages and lay in a single layer side by side — season with half the salt and pepper.

Drizzle with olive oil, lemon juice, thyme, and the staying salt and pepper. Thoroughly fold up each side of the foil sheets to produce a package around the salmon and location in a single layer on a baking sheet.

Get rid of from the oven and carefully open each packet, be cautious of the steam launched as soon as opened! Sprinkle lemon zest and parsley on top. Serve and enjoy!

Treat Almond Butter and Banana Sandwiches SmartPoints (Freestyle): 5.

Almond Butter and Banana Sandwiches.

Sugars: 8g

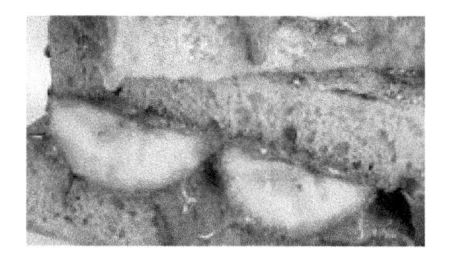

Ingredients.

1 banana, sliced.

1 Tbsp natural almond butter (enough for a dab in each sandwich).

1 Tbsp coconut flakes, unsweetened and no sulfites.

1 Tbsp cacao nibs, (optional).

Dash of cinnamon, (optional).

Add a dash of cinnamon to each bite before closing the sandwich with 1-2 granules himalayan sea salt to each (optional).

Guidelines.

Peel and slice the banana. Add almond butter and coconut together with other active ingredients on 4-5 of the 8-10 slices.

Close the sandwiches, and place the sandwiches on a plate or cookie sheet and place into the freezer. Allow the sandwiches to set for 20-30 minutes (or more), then serve and take pleasure in!


Day 12 (22 SmartPoints).

Breakfast: Tomato, Ham, and Poached Egg English Muffin SmartPoints (Freestyle): 6.

Tomato, Ham, and Poached Egg English Muffin.

Yields: 4 portions

Components.

3 teaspoons olive oil.

1 tomato, cut into 4 thick circle pieces.

4 pieces low-sodium ham.

2 entire wheat English muffins, halved.

4 eggs, poached.

1/4 teaspoon coarse ground black pepper.

Instructions.

Heat 2 teaspoons of the olive oil in a skillet on medium heat. Once hot add the tomatoes and the ham and cook up until ham is golden brown on each side and tomatoes are a little soft.

Locate the ham on the muffin and top with a tomato. Locate the poached egg on top. Drizzle with the remaining teaspoon of olive oil and sprinkle with the coarse ground black pepper.

Lunch: Clean Eating Nut Butter and Jam Sandwich SmartPoints (Freestyle): 6.

Clean Eating Nut Butter and Jam Sandwich.

Cholesterol: 0 mg

2 tablespoons of your favorite tidy eating nut butter (store purchased or homemade.

1 tablespoon Polaner All Fruit Spread of choice or other fruit sweetened jam.

2 pieces entire wheat or whole grain sandwich bread.

Directions.

Spread out the nut butter on one slice of bread. Spread the jam on the other piece of bread. Put both pieces together, slice in half, and enjoy!

Supper: One Pot Turkey and Mediterranean Quinoa SmartPoints (Freestyle): 4.

One Pot Turkey and Mediterranean Quinoa.

Servings Size: 1 cup

Ingredients.

1 tablespoon additional virgin olive oil.

2 cups nitrate totally free turkey rope sausage, cut into 1 inch portions.

2 clove garlic, minced.

1 small yellow onion, cut into strips.

1 cup low sodium chicken broth.

1 (14 ounces) can diced tomatoes.

1/2 teaspoon Kosher salt.

1 1/2 cups quinoa, rinsed in cool water.

2 cups spinach, chopped.

1/2 cup low fat feta cheese, collapsed.

Directions.

In a big skillet, heat oil on medium heat. Stir in broth, tomatoes, salt, and quinoa. Spoon into serving bowls and sprinkle with feta.

Snack: Cranberry Pumpkin Seed Granola SmartPoints (Freestyle): 6.

Cranberry Pumpkin Seed Granola.

Serving Size: 1/2 cup

4 cups rolled oats.

1 cup raw pumpkin seeds.

1/2 cup flax seed.

1/4 cup sesame seeds.

3 teaspoons cinnamon.

1/3 cup honey.

1/4 cup pure maple syrup.

1/4 cup sunflower oil.

1 tsp vanilla.

1 cup dried cranberries, (optional dried raisins, cherries or apricots).

Directions.

Preheat oven to 250 degrees Fahrenheit and prepare 2 baking sheets with parchment paper.

In a big bowl, gently mix the oats, pumpkin seeds, flax, sesame and cinnamon. To this mixture, add the honey, vanilla, syrup, and oil and stir till well-combined.

Spread the mix on the baking sheets and cook for 60 -75 minutes. To accomplish and even color on the granola while baking, stir every 15 minutes.

Remove granola and enable to cool before adding the dried cranberries. Store in an air-tight container.

Day 13 (26 SmartPoints).

Breakfast: Slow Cooker Sweet Potato Oatmeal SmartPoints (Freestyle): 6.

Sweet Potato Oatmeal.

KEEP IN MIND: The carbs in this recipe are complicated carbohydrates that are stored and used as energy that lasts all day and are discovered mainly in the oats and sweet potato. Easy carbs trigger an immediate spike in blood sugar and can be discovered in foods like pastries and candy.

Carbohydrates: 45 g

1 cup of steel cut oats.

2 cups low-fat milk.

2 cups water.

1 cup grated sweet potato, or 1/2 cup prepared and mashed sweet potato.

2 tablespoons unrefined sweetener, more or less to taste, I used coconut palm sugar. Other options: sucanat, honey or 100% pure maple syrup.

Kosher or sea salt to taste.

1/2 teaspoon cinnamon.

1 teaspoon pumpkin pie spice.

Instructions.

Combine all components in the slow cooker, cover and cook on low 2 to 2 1/2 hours, or until desired consistency is reached. Advise 4-5 quart slow cooker.

Include diced nuts and raisins if wanted.

RANGE TOP METHOD: Add all components to a medium saucepan, bring to a boil, minimize heat to a simmer and cook around 20 - 25 minutes, or till wanted consistency has actually been reached.

Lunch: Chickpea and Tomato Salad SmartPoints (Freestyle): 5.

Chickpea and Tomato Salad.

Protein: 6g.

Active ingredients.

1 (14 ounces) can chickpeas drained and rinced.

1/4 cup basil leaves, approximately sliced.

1 tablespoon olive oil.

1 little yellow onion, sliced thin.

6 big tomatoes, sliced into 1/2 inch thick wedges.

1/2 teaspoon Kosher salt.

1 tablespoon dark balsamic vinegar.

Guidelines.

In a big bowl, combine all active ingredients and toss well guaranteeing all active ingredients are covering in the oil and vinegar. Let rest, covered, in the refrigerator for 20 minutes. Toss before serving and enjoy!

Supper: Easy Chicken Bruschetta Casserole SmartPoints (Freestyle): 8.

Easy Chicken Bruschetta Casserole|Bruschetta Chicken Recipes.

Calories: 463

Ingredients.

2 1/2 cups herb seasoned bread crumbs (we utilized Pepperidge Farm's Herb Seasoned stuffing mix).

1/2 cup fat-free chicken broth (optional water).

1 (15-ounce) can petit diced tomatoes.

1.5 pounds chicken breast filets, cut into little bite size pieces.

1/2 teaspoon garlic powder.

1/2 teaspoon black pepper.

1/2 teaspoon salt.

1 1/2 teaspoons dried oregano.

1 cup part-skim mozzarella.

Instructions.

Preheat oven to 400 degrees.

In a mixing bowl integrate bread crumbs, chicken broth, and diced tomatoes with liquid set aside.

In a 9 x, 13-inch casserole pan include chicken pieces, garlic powder, pepper, salt, oregano, and 3/4 cup cheese, toss to integrate.

Add bread crumb mix and spread equally over chicken. Sprinkle with the staying cheese.

Bake for 35 minutes, or up until the chicken is done.

Treat Chocolate Peanut Butter Protein Smoothie SmartPoints (Freestyle): 7.

Chocolate Peanut Butter Protein Smoothie.

Salt: 57 mg

2 tablespoons of cocoa powder.

3 tablespoons natural peanut butter (optional, natural Powdered Peanut Butter which is much lower in fat & calories than regular peanut butter.).

1 cup low-fat milk, (optional, almond or soy milk).

1 frozen banana, pre-sliced.

1/2 cup plain Greek yogurt, fat-free.

2 tablespoons coconut palm sugar, honey is optional.

1/2 teaspoon pure vanilla extract.

ice as needed.

Instructions.

Integrate all active ingredients in a mixer and mix until smooth. Add ice according to the desired density.

Day 14 (14 SmartPoints).

Breakfast: Crustless Spinach Quiche with Sundried Tomatoes SmartPoints (Freestyle): 4.

Crustless Spinach Quiche with Sun-Dried Tomatoes.

Cholesterol: 189mg

Components.

Quiche.

6 eggs.

6 egg whites.

2 cups loosely packed spinach, coarsely chopped.

1/4 cup freshly grated parmesan cheese.

1/2 cup chopped sun-dried tomatoes without any liquid (reconstituted according to package instructions, if essential).

1/2 cup sliced onion.

1 clove garlic, minced.

1 tablespoon olive oil.

1/4 teaspoon kosher or sea salt.

1/4 teaspoon black pepper.

Crust (optional).

3/4 cups whole wheat pastry flour.

1/4 cup oat flour using 1/4 cup rolled oats * see directions.

1/4 teaspoon kosher or sea salt.

1/3 cup coconut oil, strong and cold but scoopable, refrigerate prior (optional, pure unsalted butter).

2- 3 tablespoons ice cold water.

2 tablespoons walnut pieces, optional.

Guidelines.

Preheat oven to 375 degrees.

For the crust:

Place rolled oats in a food mill or mixer and pulse up until a coarse flour is created.

Mix together the oat flour with the entire wheat flour and salt. Add the coconut oil in small pieces at a time.

Blend with a pastry cutter or hands or pulse in the food mill till pea like crumbles remain in the crust. Add the water in little quantities up until dough is the best consistency: Dough should be pretty shaggy and dry but come together when pinched in between the forefinger and thumb.

Form the dough into a ball. Wrap tightly in cling wrap and cool for 30 minutes and as much as 24 hours. Do not stress if the dough is shaggy; it will come together more after refrigeration. Roll dough out onto a floured work surface. Location the quiche/pie pan on top of the dough, upside down, and cut a circle. Carefully turn over and push the dough into the pie pan and cut the edges.

Utilize a fork to crimp the external edges of the crust or use fingers and fold over edges. Include the quiche mixture (dish listed below).

For the quiche filling:

Heat onion and garlic in a skillet with olive oil for about 5 minutes, till onion is softened and translucent. Add spinach and cook, simply up until wilted.

On the other hand, beat/whisk egg whites until very frothy. Whisk whole eggs in a different bowl. Integrate the eggs and whites. Add parmesan cheese, pepper, and salt. Fold in the spinach tomato mix and put into the pie shell — Bake for 25 minutes or until embed in the center and golden at the edges.

If desired, spray with walnut pieces 5 minutes before removing from the oven.

Lunch: Chicken Burrito Bowl SmartPoints (Freestyle): 4.

Chicken Burrito Bowl with Fresh Pico de Gallo & Creamy Chipotle Sauce.

Serving Size: 1 bowl

Ingredients.

For the Chipotle Sauce:

1/4 cup plain fat-free Greek yogurt.

1 tablespoon lime juice.

2 teaspoons canned chipotle peppers, pureed.

For the Pico de Gallo:

1/2 cup roma tomatoes, diced.

1 tablespoon red onion, diced.

1 tablespoon lime juice.

1 tablespoon jalapeno peppers, minced.

1 clove garlic, minced.

1 tablespoon fresh cilantro, sliced.

1/4 teaspoon Kosher salt.

For the Burrito Bowl:

1/2 tablespoon olive oil.

1/2 cup boneless and skinless chicken breast, sliced fine.

1 teaspoon chili powder.

1/2 teaspoon ground cumin.

3 teaspoons lime juice.

1/2 cup baby arugula.

1/2 cup baby spinach.

1 cup romaine lettuce, chopped.

1/2 cup corn kernels.

1/2 cup black beans (canned or cooked).

1/4 cup fresh avocado, pit got rid of, peeled, and mashed.

Directions.

For the Chipotle Sauce:

Integrate all active ingredients. Stir till blended well and smooth. Set aside.

For the Pico de Gallo:

Integrate all components. Mix well and set aside.

For the Burrito Bowl:

As soon as hot, include the chicken, chili powder, and cumin. Remove from heat and toss the chicken in 2 teaspoons of the lime juice and set aside.

In a bowl, toss together the lettuce, arugula and spinach. Divide the greens between 2 big serving bowls.

Next, divide the chicken in half and place the chicken over the greens in it's own section, and last the fresh pico de gallo.

Sprinkle the chipotle sauce over the top. Serve.

Dinner: Mediterranean Greek Salmon with Orzo SmartPoints (Freestyle): 3.

Mediterranean Greek Salmon with Orzo Recipe.

Sugar: 2g

Active ingredients.

1 tablespoon lemon enthusiasm.

2 teaspoons dried oregano.

1 tablespoon olive oil, divided.

4 (4 ounces) salmon filets.

1 teaspoon salt.

1/2 teaspoon black pepper.

2 cups vegetable broth.

1/2 cup whole wheat orzo.

1 cup cherry tomatoes, cut in half.

2 cups baby spinach, roughly sliced.

1/4 cup feta cheese crumbles.

Guidelines.

Preheat oven to 375 degrees and spray a baking sheet with non-stick spray.

In a small mixing bowl, combine lemon passion, dried oregano and olive oil.

Location salmon portions on the ready baking and brush olive oil lemon mix on each.

Season salmon with salt and pepper.

Prepare salmon for 15-20 minutes or up until firm and flaky.

While salmon is cooking, bring vegetable broth to a boil. Stir in the orzo and minimize to a simmer — Cook and cover for about 10 minutes or until tender.

Once the pan is hott, include the tomatoes and spinach. Saute for 5 to 10 minutes or till spinach is wilted.

put the prepared orzo and veggies on a serving plate and the salmon over the top. Sprinkle with feta cheese.

Snack: 6-Ingredient Tuna Salad Stuffed Eggs SmartPoints (Freestyle): 3.

6-Ingredient Tuna Salad Stuffed Eggs.

Calories: 118

Components.

4 large eggs.

1 (5 ounces) can tuna in water, drained pipes.

1/2 cup diced red pepper.

1/4 cup sliced green olives, drained pipes.

1/4 cup carefully chopped celery.

1/2 teaspoon sea salt.

Instructions.

Put the eggs in a little pot and cover with cold water. Bring to a boil, switch off the heat, and cover.

Let represent 10 minutes, drain, and cool.

Add tuna, peppers, olives, celery, and salt to a big bowl and stir.

Cut in half and remove the yolks; rough chop and include to the tuna mix when eggs are cool.

Carefully spoon the mixture into the egg whites, and chill until prepared to serve.

Week 3

Day 15 (16 SmartPoints).

Breakfast: Protein Salmon and Eggs on Toast SmartPoints (Freestyle): 3.

Protein Salmon and Eggs on Toast.

Dietary Fiber: 3 g

2 (4-ounce) slices nitrate-free smoked salmon/lox, sliced.

4 eggs.

1/4 cup milk.

1/4 cup chopped dill for garnish (optional).

4 pieces of entire wheat or whole grain toast.

1/4 teaspoon salt and pepper.

Instructions.

Whisk the eggs and milk together vigorously up until incorporated and frothy. Include eggs to a nonstick pan, sprayed with cooking oil, over medium heat, and enable to set a bit on the bottom, then push an edge of the eggs into the center of the pan and permit the liquid eggs on top to slide into the edges of the pan. Continue to rise the edges and stir gently to form big curds. Do not over stir the eggs.

Leading toast with rushed eggs, sliced smoked salmon, season with salt and pepper, and serve.

Lunch: Southwest Chicken Casserole with Black Beans Recipe SmartPoints (Freestyle): 6.

Southwest Chicken Casserole with Black Beans Recipe.

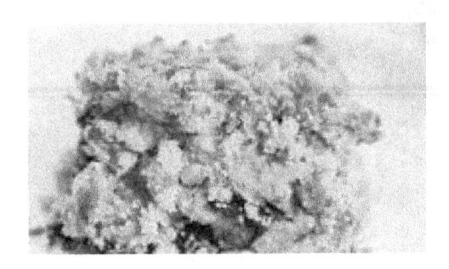

Active ingredients.

2 1/2 cups herb seasoned bread crumbs (we utilized Pepperidge Farm's classic stuffing bread crumbs).

1 1/4 cups salsa, no-sugar included.

1/2 cup water.

1.5 pounds chicken breast filets, cut into small bite size pieces.

1 teaspoon chili powder.

1 teaspoon cumin.

1/2 teaspoon black pepper.

1/2 teaspoon salt.

1 cup shredded Mexican design cheese.

1 (15 ounces) can black beans, drained.

diced green onions, optional garnish.

Guidelines.

Preheat oven to 400 degrees.

Integrate bread crumbs, salsa, and water. Reserve.

In a 9 x 13-inch casserole meal, combine chicken pieces, spices, salt, pepper, 3/4 cup cheese, and black beans, toss to combine.

Add crumb mixture to the top and spread evenly, leading with staying cheese.

Bake 35 minutes, or until chicken is prepared through. Take pleasure in!

Supper: One-Skillet Chicken and Broccoli Dinner SmartPoints (Freestyle): 2.

One-Skillet Chicken and Broccoli Dinner.

Total Fat: 3g

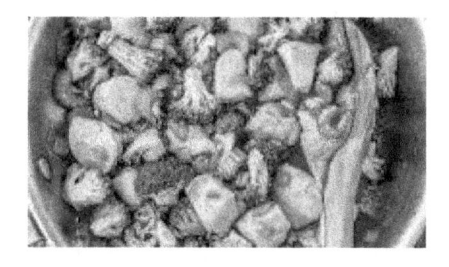

Ingredients.

Chicken and Broccoli Dinner.

1 tablespoon extra-virgin olive oil.

3 (4-6 ounce) boneless, skinless chicken breasts, sliced into large bite-sized pieces.

2 cups broccoli florets.

2 cloves garlic, minced.

1/2 cup sliced yellow onion.

1/2 cup sliced celery.

1/4 cup chicken broth, or water.

1/4 teaspoon kosher or sea salt.

1/4 teaspoon black pepper.

Sauce.

1/4 cup Coconut aminos, optional Tamari or Lite soy sauce.

2 tablespoons vegetable Sriracha.

Guidelines.

Include olive oil to a skillet over medium heat and brown the chicken on all sides, about 8 minutes. Eliminate the chicken and set aside. Add broccoli florets and lightly sauté till a little tender. Remove broccoli and reserved.

Add the broth (or water), chicken, and broccoli back to the frying pan along with the salt and pepper. Cook components for about 5 more minutes, until chicken, is heated up through.

For the sauce, blend together ingredients and contribute to the pan for the eleventh hour of cooking time. Serve and delight in!

Treat No-Bake Lemon Berry Cups SmartPoints (Freestyle): 5.

No-Bake Lemon Berry Cups.

Yields: 6 portions

Components.

1 cup Greek yogurt, fat-free.

1/2 cup (low-fat) cream cheese, softened.

Juice and zest of 1 lemon.

2 tablespoons coconut sugar or raw sugar.

1/4 cup chopped pecans.

2 large pitted dates.

1 cup fresh combined berries.

Directions.

Beat the yogurt with the cream cheese, lemon juice, enthusiasm and sugar up until fluffy and velvety.

Include dates and pecans to a food processor and process until crumb consistency.

Lay the yogurt, nuts, and fresh berries in little dessert cups. Sprinkle with extra pecans and lemon enthusiasm before serving.

Day 16 (22 SmartPoints).

Breakfast: Mediterranean Egg White Frittata SmartPoints (Freestyle): 5.

Mediterranean Egg White Frittata.

Sugar: 3g

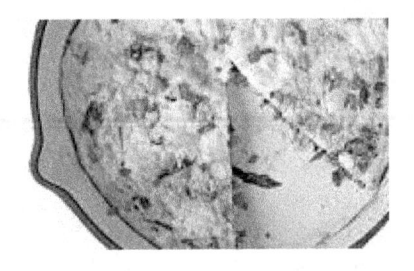

Components.

1 tablespoon olive oil.

2 tablespoons tomato, diced.

1 tablespoon red onion, diced.

2 tablespoons mushroom, diced.

1 cup spinach.

1/2 teaspoon Kosher salt.

5 egg whites.

3 tablespoons skim milk.

1/4 cup low fat feta cheese collapses.

1 teaspoon fresh oregano, chopped.

Guidelines.

Preheat oven to 450 degrees.

Heat oil on medium heat in an oven skillet. Include mushroom, onion, and tomato. Saute up until onions are soft, include spinach and salt and continue cooking up until wilted.

In a small bowl, blend together egg whites and milk. Pour egg mix over prepared vegetables. As the egg cooks, use a rubber spatula and gently lift the edge of the cooked egg to enable uncooked egg beneath. When an egg is 75% cooked, spray with feta cheese. Put in oven and bake up until egg is totally prepared and feta begins to brown - about 5 to 10 minutes. Permit to set for 5 minutes prior to serving. Sprinkle with oregano and serve.

Lunch: Veggie & Pesto Sandwich SmartPoints (Freestyle): 8.

Vegetable & Pesto Sandwich.

Ingredients.

8 ounces white mushrooms, sliced.

1 tablespoon plus 2 teaspoons additional virgin olive oil.

4 1/4 pieces red bell peppers, cored, seeded, roasted.

8 pieces artisan entire grain bread.

1/4 cup low-fat shredded mozzarella cheese.

2 Roma tomatoes, thinly sliced.

1 cup packed arugula.

1/4 cup Pesto (Basil & Spinach Pesto recipe).

Directions.

Preheat oven to 375 degrees.

If roasting your own bell peppers, slice into fourths, put on a cookie sheet, drizzle with 2 teaspoons extra virgin olive oil and roast for 20 minutes. Allow cooling slightly before removing peeling. Roasted peppers can be purchased at your regional grocery.

In a little frying pan, add 1 tablespoon oil, heat to medium-low and sauté mushrooms until soft, about 8 minutes.

While mushrooms sauté, position bread cut side up on a cookie sheet, toast up until gently golden. Eliminate toast, add 1 tablespoon mozzarella, continue toasting up until cheese melts. Remove bread from oven and top with pesto, mushrooms, bell peppers, tomatoes and arugula.

Supper: Chili Lime Chicken with Mango Rice SmartPoints (Freestyle): 8.

Chili Lime Chicken with Mango Rice.

Sodium: 474 mg

Components.

2 tablespoons Olive Oil, divided (optional: avocado oil).

1 tablespoon lime zest.

2 tablespoons lime juice.

2 teaspoons ground chili powder.

2 teaspoons ground cumin.

1/2 teaspoon salt.

1/4 teaspoon ground black pepper.

4 (6 ounces) Boneless Skinless Chicken Breasts.

2 1/4 cups low-sodium chicken broth.

1 cup uncooked long grain wild rice.

1/4 cup scallions, sliced.

1 tablespoon fresh cilantro, sliced.

1 medium mango, peeled, cored, and diced small.

1/4 cup water.

1 lime, sliced into wedges.

Guidelines.

In a little bowl, integrate 1 tablespoon olive oil, half the lime zest, half the lime juice, chili powder, pepper, salt & cumin. Include the chicken breast to the lime mix and marinade for 15-20 minutes.

On the other hand, bring the chicken broth to a boil. When boiling, include the wild rice. Lower to a simmer, cover and cook for 10 to 20 minutes or up until rice is tender Stir in the staying lime passion and lime juice, scallions, cilantro and diced mango. Set aside.

Heat big skillet over medium high heat. Include remaining 1 tablespoon of olive oil.

Sear chicken on both sides, about 2-3 minutes each side, guaranteeing it is golden brown and a little crisp on both sides. (Note: if utilizing a non-stick frying pan, chicken that might stay with the pan will.

" release" when it is all set to turn — no requirement to force it.

When chicken is golden brown on both sides, minimize heat to medium-low, pour in 1/4 cup water and cover.

Prepare on medium-low an extra 6-8 minutes, till breasts are prepared through and no longer pink inside. Internal temperature needs to be 165 degrees.

Divide rice among 4 plates, leading with chicken breast, and garnish with staying lime slices.

Snack: Sesame Garlic Nori Chips SmartPoints (Freestyle): 1.

Sesame Garlic Nori Chips.

Trans Fat: 0g

Components.

12 Nori Sheets.

1/4 cup water, room temperature.

2 tablespoons sesame oil.

2 teaspoons garlic powder.

1/4 teaspoon cayenne pepper.

1 teaspoon Kosher salt.

1 tablespoon sesame seeds.

Directions.

Preheat oven to 275 degrees. Line a baking sheet with parchment paper and set aside.

Lay 6 of the Nori sheets on a flat surface area, shiny side facing up. As soon as the sheets of Nori are matched together, cut into 1 inch strips and cut each strip in half to create about 40 chips.

In a little bowl, combine staying active ingredients. Brush each of the cut Nori chips with the mix, finish generously. Lay flat, seasoned side up, on the prepared baking sheet.

Bake for 15 to 20 minutes up until chips have actually darkened in color. Cool completely prior to serving, shop in an airtight container at space temperature.

KEEP IN MIND: Chips may not be entirely crisp until cooled.

Day 17 (21 SmartPoints).

Breakfast: Clean Eating Refrigerator Oatmeal SmartPoints (Freestyle): 8.

Tidy Eating Refrigerator Oatmeal.

Calories: 238

1/3 cup milk.

1/4 cup old fashioned oats.

1/4 cup 2% plain Greek yogurt.

1 1/2 teaspoons chia seeds.

1 teaspoon honey or agave nectar.

1/2 teaspoon cinnamon.

1/4- 1/2 cup unsweetened applesauce or pumpkin puree.

Guidelines.

Similarly, divide the very first 6 components into two half-pint containers. Securely screw the lid onto jar, and shake to integrate. Eliminate top, include applesauce or pumpkin puree, and stir well. Cool overnight, or as much as 3 days.

Lunch: Crispy Zucchini Tacos with Chipotle Cream Recipe SmartPoints (Freestyle): 8.

Crispy Zucchini Tacos with Chipotle Cream Recipe.

Carbohydrates: 44g

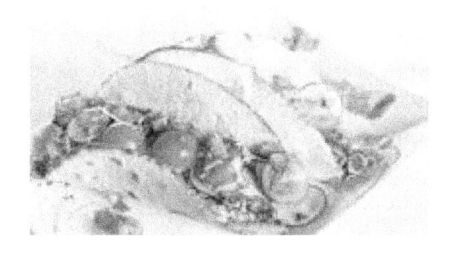

Ingredients.

For the Zucchini:

3 egg whites.

1 cup entire wheat Panko bread crumbs.

1/4 cup entire wheat flour.

2 teaspoons chili powder.

1 teaspoon ground cumin.

1/4 teaspoon Kosher salt.

1/4 teaspoon pepper.

1 big zucchini squash, cut into 1 inch long strips.

3 tablespoons coconut oil, melted.

For the Chipotle Cream:

1/2 cup plain Greek yogurt.

2 tablespoons chipotle peppers, pureed.

1 teaspoon lime juice.

For the Tacos:

12 corn tortillas.

1 cup red cabbage, shredded.

1/2 cup cherry tomatoes, cut in half.

1/2 cup radish, sliced into thin circles.

1/4 cup fresh cilantro, roughly chopped.

2 tablespoons lime juice.

Directions.

For the Zucchini:

Pre heats the oven to 400 degrees. Spray a baking sheet with non-stick spray and set aside.

put the egg whites in a bowl and carefully whip. In a 2nd bowl, integrate the Panko, flour, chili powder, salt, pepper, and cumin.

Dip the zucchini in the egg followed, however, the Panko mixture. Press the Panko into the zucchini to make sure all the sides are layered well.

Lay in a single layer on the ready flat pan and drizzle with the coconut oil — Bake for 15 to 20 minutes or till golden brown.

For the Chipotle Creme:

Whisk all active ingredients together and set aside.

For the Tacos:

Place the prepared zucchini in the bottom of each tortilla. Enjoy and serve!

Supper: Cucumber Quinoa Salad With Ground Turkey, Olives, & Feta SmartPoints (Freestyle): 2.

Cucumber Quinoa Salad With Ground Turkey, Olives, & Feta.

Calories: 97

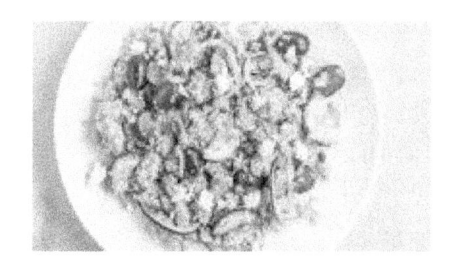

Active ingredients.

1/2 pound ground turkey sausage.

3 big cucumber, sliced into 1/4 inch half circles.

1 little red onion, sliced thin.

1 cup grape tomatoes, sliced in half.

1/2 cup kalamata olives.

1/2 cup fat totally free feta cheese collapses.

1 1/2 cup quinoa, prepared.

2 tablespoons fresh mint, chopped.

2 cloves garlic, minced.

1 tablespoon fresh oregano, sliced.

1 tablespoon lemon juice.

Directions.

In a big skillet, cook the turkey sausage. Break the sausage into small pieces as it cooks. Drain off any excess liquid and cool completely.

When the turkey sausage is cool, integrate the sausage with staying active ingredients. Mix well and chill before serving. Take pleasure in!

Snack: Peanut Butter Banana Cups SmartPoints (Freestyle): 3.

Peanut Butter Banana Cups.

Saturated Fat: 2 g

3/4 cup chocolate chips.

1 medium banana, peeled and sliced into 16 rounds.

1/4 cup natural peanut butter, shop purchased or homemade.

1 tablespoon melted coconut oil.

16 (1.25-inch) baking cups.

Instructions.

Place a sheet of wax or parchment paper on the counter top for preparation. Set the baking cups on top.

Melt chocolate in a double-boiler or in a small sauce pan over low heat. Allow cooling a little. In the meantime, integrate the melted coconut oil and peanut butter.

Include roughly 1 teaspoon melted chocolate to the bottom of each baking cup, followed by one banana piece, 1 teaspoon peanut butter mixture, and finally drop about 1/2 teaspoon melted chocolate in the center of each cup. Thoroughly location cups on a freezer safe meal or casserole pan. Cover and place in the freezer up until set, roughly 1 hour.

NOTE: Our completely portioned Peanut Butter Banana Cups thaw quickly. For best results, take pleasure in one at a time after enabling to set at space temperature level about 2-3 minutes. To avoid the peanut butter mix from softening too quickly, add 1 tablespoon powdered sugar to peanut butter and coconut oil mixture before contributing to cups.

Day 18 (18 SmartPoints).

Breakfast: Easy Turkey Burrito Skillet SmartPoints (Freestyle): 11.

Easy Turkey Burrito Skillet.

Serving Size: 1 cup

Components.

1 pound ground turkey.

1 tablespoon chili powder.

1 teaspoon ground cumin.

1 tablespoon lime juice.

1/2 teaspoon Kosher salt.

If you like it spicy!), 1/4 teaspoon ground black pepper (or crushed red pepper.

1/4 cup water.

1 cup no-sugar included chunky salsa.

1 (15 ounces) can black beans, rinsed and drained.

4 (6 inches) whole wheat flour tortillas, cut into 1 inch strips.

1 cup low-fat cheddar cheese.

1/2 cup plain Greek yogurt.

1/4 cup fresh cilantro, chopped.

Instructions.

In a big frying pan, prepare the ground turkey until cooked through, breaking up the turkey into small pieces as it cooks. Stir in the chili powder, cumin, lime juice, salt, pepper, water, salsa, and beans.

Top each serving with Greek yogurt and fresh cilantro. Enjoy and serve!

Lunch: Fiesta Chicken Soup SmartPoints (Freestyle): 1.

Slow Cooker Fiesta Chicken Soup.

Components.

1/2 cup diced onion.

1 clove garlic, minced.

1 (15 oz.) can black beans, rinsed and drained pipes.

1 (15 oz.) can kidney beans, rinsed and drained.

1 (4.5 oz.) can dice green chili peppers.

1 (14.5 oz.) can diced tomatoes.

2 1/2 cups chicken broth, low salt, fat-free (use more broth for a thinner soup).

1 cup fresh or frozen corn.

Juice from 1 lime.

1 tablespoon chili powder.

1 teaspoon cumin.

1/2 teaspoon cayenne pepper (basically to taste).

1/2 teaspoon black pepper.

Kosher or sea salt to taste.

1/2 cup newly sliced cilantro.

2 chicken breasts fillets, skinless, cut into 1-2" cubes (no requirement to pre-cook).

Directions.

Include all active ingredients to the slow cooker, stir to combine — cover and cook on low 6-8 hours.

Supper: Warm Chicken Salad Over Arugula with Creamy Dill Dressing SmartPoints (Freestyle): 1.

Warm Chicken Salad Over Arugula with Creamy Dill Dressing.

Trans Fat: 0g

Ingredients.

1 tablespoon olive oil.

2 (4 to 6 ounce) boneless and skinless chicken breast, cut into 1 inch cubes.

1 cup fresh asparagus cut into 1 inch pieces.

1/2 cup grape tomatoes, cut in half.

1/4 teaspoon Kosher salt.

1/4 teaspoon ground black pepper.

1/2 cup Greek yogurt.

1 teaspoon dry dill.

2 tablespoon lemon juice.

1 tablespoon red, white wine vinegar.

1 tablespoon Dijon mustard.

1 tablespoon entire grain mustard.

4 cups child arugula.

Directions.

When hot, include the chicken and cook for about 5 minutes or up until the chicken is about half cooked. Cook till chicken is cooked through and tomatoes are blistered about 5 more minutes.

Combine the yogurt, dill, lemon juice, vinegar, and both mustards. Mix well and set aside.

Divide arugula into serving bowls. Add about 3 tablespoons of the yogurt dressing to the warm chick and blend well to coat the chicken in the dressing. Spoon over the arugula. Drizzle with additional dressing if desired.

Treat: Clean eating Deviled Eggs SmartPoints (Freestyle): 5.

Tidy Eating Deviled Eggs.

Sugars: 1g

Active ingredients.

4 big eggs, difficult boiled and shells eliminated.

2 tablespoons tidy mayo.

1/2 teaspoon apple cider vinegar.

1/2 teaspoon yellow mustard, no sugar included.

1/8 teaspoon black pepper.

1/4 teaspoon sea salt.

1/2 teaspoon paprika for garnish.

Instructions.

Slice hard boiled eggs in half lengthwise. Eliminate yolks, including to a small mixing bowl and mash with a fork. Include the staying components, other than paprika, and stir till velvety.

Uniformly divide mixture inside the prepared egg whites. Sprinkle with paprika and refrigerate till ready to serve.

Day 19 (24 SmartPoints).

Breakfast: 2-Ingredient Sweet Potato Pancakes SmartPoints (Freestyle): 3.

2-Ingredient Sweet Potato Pancakes 3.

Trans Fat: 0g

Ingredients.

1 cup mashed sweet potato (about 2 medium potatoes, peeled, cooked, and mashed).

2 eggs.

Directions.

Integrate the sweet potato and egg. Stir well. If wanted, add 1/2 teaspoon cinnamon.

Lightly spray a skillet with non-stick spray and heat on medium heat. Pour about 1/4 cup of the batter into the pan. Cook about 3 to 4 minutes, or until pancakes begin to bubble in the.
Thoroughly flip and cook for another 2 to 3 minutes. Once prepared, get rid of pancake from the pan and repeat the process up until all the batter has been utilized. Grease the frying pan as required with non-stick spray in-between cooking the pancakes.

Serve hot, if preferred top with maple syrup, honey, coconut butter, fresh fruit, or your favorite jam!

Lunch: Avocado and Poached Egg Quinoa Bowl SmartPoints (Freestyle): 7.

Perfect Avocado and Poached Egg Quinoa Bowl.

Calories: 450

Active ingredients.

1 cup cooked quinoa (make certain it's hot!).

1 teaspoon olive oil.

1/2 teaspoon dark balsamic vinegar.

1/4 teaspoon Kosher salt.

1 cup grape tomatoes, cut in 1/2.

1/2 (15 ounces) can no salt added chickpeas, drained and rinsed.

1/2 avocado, pit removed, peeled, sliced into strips.

2 big eggs, poach (Need to understand how to poach and egg, take a look at our post How to Make Perfect Poached Eggs ).

1/4 cup fresh parsley leaves.

Directions.

In a mixing bowl, toss together the quinoa, olive oil, vinegar, salt, tomatoes, and chickpeas. Toss just to integrate all active ingredients together. Separate the mix between 2 serving bowls.

Place half of the avocado on top of the quinoa in each bowl, and put a poached egg to the side of the avocado on each bowl. Sprinkle with fresh parsley. Serve and enjoy!

Dinner: Quick & Easy Black Bean Lentil Soup SmartPoints (Freestyle): 2.

Quick & Easy Black Bean Lentil Soup.

Yields: 8 cups

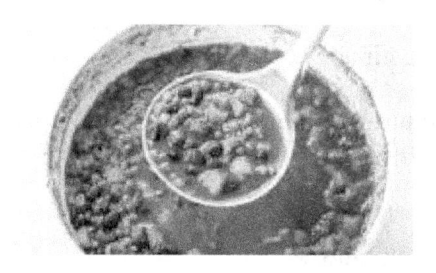

Components.

1/4 cup water.

1 sweet or yellow onion, diced.

2 carrots, carefully diced.

1 (14.5 ounces) can diced tomatoes.

1 cup dry green lentils.

2 (15 ounces) cans black beans, drained and washed.

1 teaspoon chili powder.

1 teaspoon cumin.

1/2 teaspoon black pepper.

1 teaspoon salt, more or less to taste.

1/8 teaspoon crushed red pepper flakes.

4 1/2 cups vegetable broth, optional water or a combination of the 2.

1/2 cup of canned coconut milk.

Directions.

In a big pot, over medium-low heat, add water and sauté diced onion until tender, about 8 minutes.

Add the remaining ingredients, stir and cover.

Bring soup to a boil over medium-high heat, reduce heat to a simmer, cover and cook up until lentils and carrots are tender approximately 30 minutes.

Garnish with (optional) diced avocado.


Snack: Caramel Pumpkin Spice Popcorn SmartPoints (Freestyle): 12.

Caramel Pumpkin Spice Popcorn Recipe.

Salt: 151 mg

Ingredients.

12 cups popcorn (2/3 cup kernels makes about 12 cups popcorn).

1/2 cup coconut oil.

1 cup of coconut sugar.

1/2 cup pure maple syrup.

1/2 teaspoon kosher or sea salt.

1 teaspoon pumpkin pie spice.

1/2 teaspoon baking soda.

1 teaspoon pure vanilla.

Guidelines.

Preheat oven to 225 degrees.

Include popped corn to a big mixing bowl.

In a medium saucepan, combine coconut oil, coconut sugar, maple syrup, and salt. Put over prepared popcorn and toss to coat.

Spread coated popcorn on a parchment lined big baking sheet. Bake for 1 hour, stirring every 15 minutes. Get rid of from oven and permit to cool totally before serving.

OPTIONAL: Add 1 cup combined nuts to popcorn prior to including warm maple syrup mixture.

Day 20 (27 SmartPoints).

Breakfast: French Toast Casserole SmartPoints (Freestyle): 6.

Slow Cooker French Toast Casserole.

Sugars: 19 g

Ingredients.

2 entire eggs.

2 egg whites.

1 1/2 cups 1% milk.

2 tablespoon honey.

1 teaspoon vanilla extract.

1/2 teaspoon cinnamon.

9 Slices entire grain bread.

FILLING:

3 cups finely diced uncooked apple pieces (Honey Crisp or Gala are both terrific in this recipe).

3 tablespoon honey.

1 teaspoon lemon juice.

1/3 cup diced raw pecans.

1/2 teaspoon cinnamon.

Guidelines.

Include the first 6 components to a medium blending bowl, blend to combine. Lightly spray the within the slow cooker with nonstick cooking spray.

Add all the filling ingredients in a little mixing bowl and stir to coat apple pieces, reserved.

Cut bread pieces into triangles (that's in half, just triangle shaped). Location one layer of bread (6 triangles) on the bottom of the slow cooker, add 1/4 of the filling and repeat up until there are 3 layers of bread. Include the staying filling to the top.

Put egg mixture over bread. Cover and cook on high 2 to 2-1/2 or low 4 hours, or till bread has soaked up the liquid.

3 Bananas (diced) can be an alternative to apples.

Keep in mind: Drizzle with 100% pure maple syrup if desired.

Lunch: Turkey and Spicy Hummus Club SmartPoints (Freestyle): 12.

Turkey and Spicy Hummus Club.

Carbohydrates: 34g

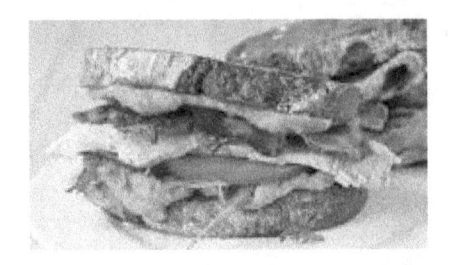

Active ingredients.

For the Hummus.

1 (15 ounces) can garbanzo beans, drained pipes and washed.

1 tablespoon tahini.

2 teaspoons lemon juice.

4 cloves garlic, minced.

2 tablespoons olive oil.

1/2 teaspoon Kosher salt.

1/2 teaspoon smoked paprika.

1/2 teaspoon cayenne pepper.

1 tablespoon jalapeno, minced.

For the Sandwich:

8 slices dark rye bread, toasted.

8 ounces thin sliced turkey.

8 slices turkey bacon, cooked and nitrate-free.

1 big tomato, sliced into rings.

1 cup infant arugula.

Instructions.

For the Hummus:

Combine all components in a food mill and mix up until smooth. If hummus is too thick, and additional lemon juice and olive oil up until wanted consistency is reached. Shop remaining hummus in an airtight container cooled.

For the Sandwiches:

On 4 pieces of the rye bread, spread out about 2 tablespoons of the humus. On top of the hummus, put the remaining components, divided equally among each piece of bread.

Supper: Clean Eating Chicken Fried Rice SmartPoints (Freestyle): 6.

Clean Eating Chicken Fried Rice.

Protein: 23g.

Ingredients.

For the rice.

1 cup long grain wild rice.

2 1/2 cups water.

1/4 teaspoon salt.

For the fried rice.

1 tablespoon olive oil.

1/2 cup chopped onions.

1 cup diced bell pepper, green or red.

1 tablespoon finely minced, peeled ginger root.

3 tablespoons water.

2 boneless, skinless chicken breasts, cut into thin strips.

2 eggs, beaten.

2-3 tablespoons lite soy sauce, optional Tamari.

2 teaspoons sesame oil.

1/4 cup chopped scallions or green onions, optional.

Instructions.

For the rice:

Include rice, water, and salt to a pot, stir once, and bring to a boil over high heat. Enable to prepare, unblemished, for 40 minutes or till tender and liquid is absorbed.

Cool rice up until cold, ideally overnight.

To fry the rice:

Add olive oil to a big nonstick frying pan or wok. Over medium heat include chicken, onions, bell pepper, and ginger and cook for about 4 to 5 minutes, till onions are clear and chicken is mostly prepared through. Add cooked rice and water and increase heat to medium-high.

Push rice to one side and include beaten eggs to the other side, scramble quickly then toss in with the rice mix. Stir in the soy sauce and sesame oil.

Eliminate from the heat and toss in the scallions, if using. Delight in!

Treat Peanut Butter Yogurt Honey Dip SmartPoints (Freestyle): 3.

Peanut Butter Yogurt Honey Dip.

Dietary Fiber: 1 g

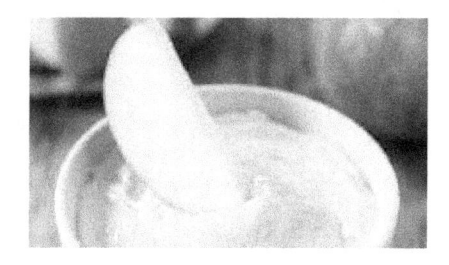

Active ingredients.

1 cup Greek yogurt, fat-free.

1/2 cup natural peanut butter.

1 tablespoon honey.

Instructions.

In a small bowl, combine all active ingredients. Serve with your favorite fruits or veggies.

Day 21 (21 SmartPoints).

Breakfast: Crustless Asparagus Quiche SmartPoints (Freestyle): 1.

Crustless Asparagus Quiche.

Protein: 7 g.

Ingredients.

2 cups sliced asparagus.

6 egg whites.

2 entire eggs.

1/3 cup diced onion.

1/2 cup (low-fat) feta cheese, optional parmesan cheese.

1/2 cup diced tomatoes.

1/4 teaspoon black pepper.

Kosher or sea salt to taste.

Instructions.

Preheat oven to 350 degrees.

Combine all active ingredients in a medium mixing bowl and put into a quiche pan or 9-inch glass pie plate.

Bake at 350 ° for around 45 minutes or up until filling is set.

Lunch: Healthiest Greek Salad SmartPoints (Freestyle): 14.

Healthiest Greek Salad.

Cholesterol: 34 mg

Ingredients.

1/4 cup extra-virgin olive oil.

2 tablespoons red wine vinegar.

1/2 teaspoon salt.

1/4 teaspoon pepper.

1 big cucumber.

1/2 cup kalamata olives.

4 large tomatoes, sliced.

1 big onion, sliced.

4 cups romaine lettuce or other green lettuce of option.

4 ounces feta cheese, diced or fallen apart.

Zest of 1 lemon.

1 teaspoon dried oregano.

Guidelines.

In a small bowl, to make the dressing, mix the extra virgin olive oil, vinegar, salt and pepper. You can adjust the quantity according to taste.

In a salad serving bowl, blend the lettuce, cucumber, olives, tomatoes, onions, feta, lemon zest and dried oregano. When ready to serve, Mix with the dressing.

Dinner: Tuna Zucchini Noodle Bake SmartPoints (Freestyle): 3.

Tuna Zucchini Noodle Bake.

Carbohydrates: 0g

Components.

4 medium zucchini, cut into noodles with a spiralizer.

2 teaspoons olive oil.

1/2 cup yellow onion, diced.

2 (6 ounces) cans water-packed flaked tuna, drained.

1 tablespoon tomato paste.

1 (15 ounces) can diced tomatoes, drained pipes.

1/2 cup skim milk.

1 teaspoon dried thyme.

1/2 teaspoon Kosher salt.

1/4 teaspoon ground black pepper.

1/4 cup grated fat-free parmesan cheese.

1/2 cup fat-free shredded cheddar cheese.

Instructions.

Preheat oven to 400 degrees, spray a 9 x 13 inch pan with nonstick spray. Spread out the spiralized zucchini in an even layer in the casserole meal. Reserve.

In a large frying pan, heat the oil, Once hot, include the onion and cook up until soft, about 2 minutes. Include the tuna and tomato paste, prepare for about 1 more minute. Stir in the diced tomatoes, milk, thyme, salt, and pepper. Bring to a simmer and stir in the parmesan till melted.

Put the tuna mix over the zucchini noodles. Sprinkle with cheddar cheese on top. Bake, exposed, for 15 minutes or until cheese is melted and bubbly.


Treat Classic Cucumber and Tomato Salad SmartPoints (Freestyle): 3.

Traditional Cucumber & Tomato Salad.

Protein: 1 g.

Ingredients.

2 medium cucumbers, peeled and very finely sliced.

2 cups grape or cherry tomatoes, a piece in half lengthwise.

1/2 red onion, very finely sliced.

1/4 teaspoon black pepper.

Kosher or sea salt to taste.

2 tablespoons fresh Dill.

2 tablespoons white balsamic vinegar.

1 tablespoon Extra-Virgin Olive Oil.

1 teaspoon yellow or Dijon Mustard, no sugar included.

1 teaspoon honey, (optional).

Guidelines.

In a large salad bowl integrate cucumbers, tomatoes and onion. Whisk together the remaining ingredients and pour over cucumber mix, toss to coat. Serve immediately.

# PROS AND CONS OF WEIGHT WATCHERS LIFESTLE

Pros

Flexible and well balanced

Weight Watchers uses one of the most versatile business diets on the market. By designating veggies, fruits, and lean proteins a worth of no points, the diet motivates you to make these the bulk of your meals while still allowing for sufficient grains and dairy within your day-to-day SmartPoints allotment.

Teaches Lifelong Skills

No matter what diet plan you pick, you desire it to be something you can follow for life. Weight Watchers teaches essential healthy eating abilities that will serve you well over time - like determining your parts and serving sizes and encouraging you to prepare food at home.

No Foods are Forbidden

There is no list of foods to prevent on Weight Watchers as you'll discover on other diet plans. Instead, you'll count SmartPoints and make FitPoints. As soon as in a while, the point system motivates you to eat healthy food, however, also allows you to indulge with sweet snacks or treats.

Slow and Steady Weight Loss

You can expect to lose one to 2 pounds a week on Weight Watchers. A number of research studies have actually supported these claims and shown the program to be effective for weight-loss

For example, one study released in 2017 in Lancet compared weight loss among those using self-help products, Weight Watchers for 12 weeks, or Weight Watchers for 52 weeks. The 52-week program led to much better outcomes than the 12-week program, and the 12-week program had much better results than the self-guided program.

Another 2015 organized review in Annals of internal medicine analyzed several business weight-loss programs. The research study discovered that those on Weight Watchers lost 2.6 percent more weight compared to manage groups.2.

Interestingly, a causal sequence may also exist for spouses of those taking part in Weight Watchers (or other weight-loss programs). A study published in 2018 in Obesity found substantial weight-loss amongst spouses of those taking part in Weight Watchers, although they themselves did not sign up with.3.

Heaps of Support and Resources.

Weight Watchers offers more resources than most other diet plan programs. You'll find the app and site convenient for computing and tracking SmartPoints, in addition to discovering recipe concepts.

If you like accountability and group support, you can likewise attend the routine group conferences. You can even register for a premium subscription that consists of customized coaching for one-on-one assistance.

Also, if you own a Fitbit for weight reduction, or utilize another gadget or weight reduction app like Jawbone, Withings, Misfit, Garmin Vivofit, Apple Health, or Map-My-Run, you can sync your activity to Weight Watchers. This assists you handle all your exercise and weight loss information in one place.

Decreases Diabetes Risk.

Due to the fact that Weight Watchers guides users towards nutritious alternatives and helps individuals slim down, the program has actually been associated with a decreased danger of type 2 diabetes or much better blood sugar level control amongst those with diabetes.

A study published in 2017 in BMJ open diabetes research study & care looked at the results of referring those with pre-diabetes to a complimentary Weight Watchers program. Those who took part lost weight and reduced hemoglobin A1c levels (a step of blood sugar control). In reality, 38 percent of patients returned to totally regular blood glucose metrics.4.

Other studies have actually found comparable outcomes amongst those with pre-diabetes, including a research study released in BMJ Open Diabetes Research and Care in 2017.5 Another research study released in 2016 in Obesity (Silver Springs) has likewise revealed those who already have diabetes skilled weight loss and better blood sugar level control when following the Weight Watchers program.6.

Promotes Exercise.

The Weight Watchers system motivates lots of everyday motion and workout. You earn FitPoints with the motion that assist you to stabilize your food consumption. Guidance is provided for new exercisers and for those who can exercise harder and burn more calories.

Even though there are many benefits to Weight Watchers, that does not mean it's the ideal suitable for everyone. Think about the drawbacks before purchasing the plan.

Cons

Can Be Costly

The cost for Weight Watchers will differ from individual to individual, depending upon the alternatives you choose and for how long you'd like to remain on the program. Make sure to consider the overall cost for the whole time you require to be on the plan to make certain that you can manage it.

Digital-only programming is the least expensive alternative, while in-person workshops fall in the middle, and personalized training will cost the many. Present rates range from around $4 weekly on the low end for the online program, to around $14 each week for customized coaching.

You can get somewhat discounted weekly rates by paying up front for numerous months, or by keeping an eye out for promos. Some medical insurance companies also offer a discount for Weight Watchers, so make sure to talk to yours if you're preparing to sign up with.

Just just how much does it cost on average for people to reach their goals? In a research study that examined the cost for a group of women to lose 5 percent of their body weight, they discovered Weight Watchers clocked in at roughly $1,610. While this might sound like a lot, believe of the cost-savings that might come later on with better total health. This quantity was still far less than the other weight loss program studied, Curves Complete, which clocked in at $8,613 to achieve the exact same objectives.

Counting Points Can Be Tedious

If you do not like counting calories, you may not like counting SmartPoints either. The procedure can be time-consuming and may be too made complex for people who want a basic and quick technique for consumtion.

Weekly Weigh-Ins Are Necessary

You require to weigh in as soon as a week to track your development on Weight Watchers. For some individuals, this requirement is unpleasant. You might not like to be weighed in at a group meeting (although the weigh in just happens in front of the leader, not the entire group). Or you might get annoyed by lack of progress on the scale that week, despite the fact that you followed your plan precisely.

For others, though, weekly weigh-ins can be a plus, assisting in keeping an eye on development and remaining on the best track.

Minimal Evidence for Cardiovascular Benefits

A methodical evaluation in 2016 found that Weight Watchers provided little additional aid for blood pressure or cholesterol compared to control groups-- though data was restricted.7 If you're searching for a diet with recognized cardiovascular advantages, you might desire to investigate other choices (like the Mediterranean diet plan, for example).

## Too Much Freedom

As ridiculous as it sounds, too much freedom can be an Achilles heel for some people. If that speaks to your personality, weight loss prepares with stricter guidelines may work better.

## May Lead to Unhealthy Dieting

There is some concern that the focus on counting points can result in an unhealthy relationship with food. There have been anecdotal reports that some Weight Watchers fans "save up" points to binge on food later on. Though they might not surpass their daily points, that behavior does breech on unhealthy dieting.

# BENEFITS

Weight Watchers prides itself on being an adaptable and versatile way to slim down or loss weight.

The SmartPoints system motivates members to make clever, healthy choices.

It likewise enables members to enjoy their preferred foods, as long as they fit into their allotted day-to-day points.

Unlike diets that prohibited specific foods, Weight Watchers permits users to indulge within factor.

This means members can go out to dinner or attend a celebration without stressing if the food served will suit their diet plan.

Plus, Weight Watchers is an excellent option for people with dietary constraints, like vegans or those with food allergic reactions, because members select how they spend their SmartPoints.

Weight Watchers worries part control and the importance of exercise, which are important to weight-loss success.

Another advantage of the program is that it offers members with a large assistance system.

Online members take advantage of 24/7 chat support and an online community, while those who attend weekly conferences remain inspired by engaging with fellow members.

What's more, Weight Watchers uses magazines and newsletters for members.

Weight Watchers enables dieters to be flexible with their food options and has lots of benefits, consisting of a large support system.

# THINGS YOU MIGHT NOT KNOW ABOUT WEIGHT WATCHERS

Gadgets like the Fitbit have actually chewed into their market share. Weight Watchers remains a formidable presence in the $72 billion weight loss industry. Unlike numerous crash diet and suspicious supplements, there's actual clinical evidence that states the program-- which combines caloric control with social support-- works. Recently, the company has expanded to include guidance on total wellness and has actually changed its name to its initials: WW. Present CEO Mindy Grossman thinks the program will keep its prominent function as a leader in weight management. Have a look at these truths about points, spokespeople, and the function of animal organs in a balanced diet.

## 1. THE FOUNDER OF WEIGHT WATCHERS WAS MISTAKEN FOR A PREGNANT WOMAN

When 37-year-old Queen's homemaker Jean Nidetch strolled into a grocery store in 1962, she faced a next-door neighbor who matched her on her appearance. Prior to Nidetch could thank her, the neighbor asked when she was due. Unsatisfied with both the social synthetic pas and her weight of 214 pounds, Nidetch chose to go on a diet plan and checked out the New York Board of Health for guidance. After cutting out soda and consuming more protein, Nidetch lost 20 pounds in 10 weeks. she started meeting buddies to exchange stories about food temptations. One confessed to consuming a donut out of a trash can. A movement was born.

## 2. THE FIRST WEIGHT WATCHERS MEETINGS WERE HELD OVER A PIZZA PARLOR.

When Nidetch (who ultimately lost 70 pounds and kept it off) understood there was a need for meetings beyond her circle of buddies, she started Weight Watchers as an incorporated business in 1963. Those early conferences were kept in an empty area over a New York pizza parlor; the owner was puzzled regarding why there was a line of individuals outside who never ever stopped in for a piece.

## 3. THE ORIGINAL WEIGHT WATCHERS PLAN CALLED FOR LIVER AND BRAINS.

Weight Watchers invested its very first decades endorsing a limited-quantities program, which didn't count calories; however, restricted members to specific kinds of foods. The diet plan also welcomed frankfurters.

## 4. WEIGHT WATCHERS USED TO BE OWNED BY HEINZ.

You probably don't think about slathering your meals in sugar-laden condiments when you believe of shedding pounds. But when Nidetch's meetings grew from community chats to public assemblies, it caught the attention of the H.J. Heinz company, the ketchup manufacturer. Heinz bought Weight Watchers for $71 million in 1978; they sold business off to a European investment firm in 1999, but maintained a small stake and still distribute frozen foods bearing the Weight Watchers brand name.

## 5. WEIGHT WATCHERS MAGAZINE WAS FOR "ATTRACTIVE PEOPLE."

The Weight Watchers motion has bled into frozen foods, apps, and other licensed items, but one of their most long-lasting tie-ins has been Weight Watchers publication. When the publication first appeared on newsstands in 1968, it provided basic food tips and way of life recommendations. In 1975, editors (consisting of Matty Simmons, who would later found National Lampoon) added the subtitle Magazine For Attractive People.

## 6. WEIGHT WATCHERS MESSED WITH SUCCESS. TWO TIMES.

Weight Watchers had long been a program based on social assistance and dietary suggestions. It wasn't up until 1997, when the company debuted its "Points" system, that the brand name ended up being a cultural phenomenon. By designating indicate a wide variety of store-bought and restaurant foods, program members related to options like a banana (now allowed) or cupcake as being worth a particular variety of points. As long as they didn't exceed their overall allowance for the day, they'd reduce weight. The revamped PointsPlus, presented in 2010, recognized 200 calories of protein and 200 calories of baked goods were indeed various and shifted their mathematical worths appropriately.

## 7. NOT EVERYONE WAS HAPPY ABOUT THE WEIGHT WATCHERS to CHANGE.

On then-CEO David Kirchhoff's blog, posters grumbled that the brand-new system overthrew their comfort level with what had actually come before. "I hate it," one member composed. "I hate discovering the new points and losing all the foods that I've put in over the last 3 years. I'm totally annoyed that microwave popcorn is three points now !!!!".

## 8. WEIGHT WATCHERS MIGHT COST YOU $75 A POUND.

The Duke-National University of Singapore did a little number-crunching in 2014 and discovered that, with approximately $377 in annual membership fees and roughly five pounds lost per year, Weight Watchers costs members about $75 for every single disappearing pound. But it's still a more affordable alternative than Jenny Craig, which demands members purchase the business's own food at the cost of approximately $2,500 annually. At a typical 16 pounds lost, that's roughly double the cost.

## 9. WEIGHT WATCHERS IS CONFIDENT YOU WON'T ABUSE YOUR FREE FRUIT PRIVILEGES.

Under the PointsPlus system, members get a free pass with vegetables and fruits: they relate to absolutely no points. While some diet professionals and nutritional experts argue that consuming too much fruit might literally tip the scales, Kirchhoff discussed that "There's so little proof that people abuse fruit. It takes a while to eat. It's filling. Could you consume 12 bananas and count it as zero points? Yes. However, how would you feel later?".

## 10. CHARLES BARKLEY WAS CAUGHT DISSING WEIGHT WATCHERS.

Among many celebrity endorsers, Charles Barkley (a.k.a. "The Round Mound of Rebound") became a spokesman in 2011. According to the New York Daily News, he was revealing an NBA game in January 2012 and-- not realizing his microphone was still live-- stated his offer with Weight Watchers to be a "fraud." He was apparently referring to getting paid to drop weight, not the program itself; the business later said in a declaration they "love Charles ... he's unfiltered.".

11. WEIGHT WATCHERS REALLY HAD TO WORK FOR CHINA.

Kirchhoff visited China in 2011 to see how the culture was embracing the Points system. Due to the fact that pre-packaged food has complicated, extra labeling, and because the Chinese often eat in restaurants, the business had to wait while chefs made nearly 20,000 common dishes and then measured their nutritional content.

12. You can attend conferences in New Zealand.

Now, a little over half a century after it started, you can find a Weight Watchers meeting quite much throughout the United States-- however, it's not just limited to North America. Weight Watchers has programs in 20 nations, including Brazil, France, and South Africa. If you're attempting to get support while traveling abroad, you can drop into a conference and perhaps even satisfy some locals.

13. There are more than 36,000 conferences a week.

That's a lot of conferences-- and a heck of a great deal of support. Members talk about healthy eating tips, exercise, and behavioral changes that are required for obtaining a healthier way of life.

14. It has more members than many significant cities have homeowners.

While your preferred celeb might be consuming lemon and cayenne or doing 30-day juice cleans, it's clear that those diet plans aren't practical for the majority of people. Weight Watchers has over a million members-- that's more than the population of San Francisco!

15. The famous Points system is reasonably new.

Points, the system that Weight Watchers is now most famous for, where dieters are allocated a particular variety of points for food and workout, was in fact presented in 1997. Now, when you stroll into any supermarket, there make certain to be products with the Points label on them-- no more uncertainty required.

16. Its brand name ambassadors have varied from royals to tv moguls.

You might have seen ads featuring celebrities Jennifer Hudson and Jessica Simpson. Did you know its most popular spokesperson, Duchess of York Sarah Ferguson, backed the brand name for an outstanding 11 years? In fact, she when told the Telegraph that the program "literally conserved [ her] life." Now, American television royalty has joined the motion, with Oprah just recently revealing her collaboration with Weight Watchers.

17. It's not simply for ladies.

"Men do not talk about dieting and losing weight, but they should," Barkley said of the program. "Losing weight is much better if you've got people around you who can keep you inspired.".

18. Weight Watchers was ranked as the top weight reduction program of 2015.

According to a ranking done by U.S. News with a panel of health and nutrition professionals, Weight Watchers is the top diet program for weight reduction in the United States based on effectiveness, health dangers, and ease. And on top of that, it's lucrative: in 2014, the Wall Street Journal reported that the business made a whopping $30.8 million.

19. It was spoofed on Saturday Night Live.

This classic act from 1991 stars Designing Women's Delta Burke along with SNL heavyweights like Chris Farley, Al Franken, and Jan Hooks. Hilariously area on, it pokes fun at the program's "sharing your development" conference design.

20. Your average weight loss per month depends upon how frequently you appear.

A 2010 research study published in the American Journal of Lifestyle Medicine revealed that participants who participated in at least two-thirds of their conferences over the course of 6 months showed the most success in their weight loss goals, losing 14 pounds and experiencing a "remarkable change" in their glucose and insulin levels. In other words, working the program assists the program work for you.

21. It's officially gone digital.

Much unaffiliated business has attempted to produce companion apps for the program, but Weight Watchers now has an official method to help you track your Points and health wirelessly. The business associated Philips to introduce ActiveLink 2.0, a wearable and syncable screen that tracks your activity and sleeps so you will not overestimate your workout output-- and therefore won't unintentionally eat method more than you should.

## 22. SOME PEOPLE ARE BANNED FROM WEIGHT WATCHERS.

Not from consuming sensibly, undoubtedly, but from actively getting involved in the Weight Watchers neighborhood. Demographics that are warned against taking part in their programs include anyone under the age of 18 unless those 13 and older have composed permission from a health care company; anyone suffering from anorexia nervosa or bulimia nervosa, and anybody pregnant.

## CONCLUSION

Weight Watchers is a popular weight-loss program that draws in hundreds of thousands of new members every year.

Its flexible, points-based system attracts numerous dieters and stresses the importance of living a healthy lifestyle.

Research studies have actually discovered that Weight Watchers is a reliable way to drop weight and keep it off.

If you're looking for an evidence-based weight-loss program that lets you indulge in your favorite foods once in a while, Weight Watchers might help you reach your health and health goals.

**Do Not Go Yet; One Last Thing To Do**

If you enjoyed this book or found it useful, I'd be very grateful if you'd post a short review on Amazon. Your support does make a difference, and I read all the reviews personally so I can get your feedback and make this book even better.

*Thanks again for your support!*

CPSIA information can be obtained
at www.ICGtesting.com
Printed in the USA
BVHW011746030121
596874BV00006B/26

9 781801 208857